MADNESS
OF THE
XX
CENTURY

A TESTIMONY

Zbigniew Marian Haszlakiewicz

PAGE PUBLISHING
Conneaut Lake, PA

First originally published by Page Publishing 2023
First self-published in 1998 by Z.M.H.

ISBN 979-8-88654-372-8 (pbk)
ISBN 979-8-88654-380-3 (digital)

Printed in the United States of America

Contents

Prologue and Acknowledgments

With the terrible time of World War II drifting slowly into history, more and more misrepresentations influence people's memory about the events that shocked the world. Nobody seems to remember Hitler's declaring in his *Mein Kampf* that the Germanic race is superior to any other and his laying out a plan of subordination or destruction of every nation, which would oppose Nazi rulers. Nobody seems to remember, either, Marx, Lenin, and Stalin proclaiming social hatred and mercilessly annihilating anybody who would not accept Soviet Communist rule.

Now, in the last decade of the twentieth century, whenever an American notices the number tattooed on my left underarm and learns that it is a prisoner registration number of the Auschwitz concentration camp, he would be astounded and would start asking questions, which would show his limited knowledge of the subject. A young one would ask, "What's that camp?" Another one, middle-aged, would say, "How come? You are not a Jew!" And still another, the oldest, would wonder, "How did you survive?"

Perhaps the following pages, written strictly from my memory, will provide some answers to all these questions. Only the maps and site plans are not drawn from memory. Those related to Auschwitz were taken from the book *Oświęcim: Hitlerowski Obóz Masowej Zagłady*, published in 1987 by Wydawnictwo Interpress in Warsaw, Poland, whereas those related to Dora were taken from the book *Kryptonim Dora* by Czerniecki and Z. Zonik, published in 1973 by Książka i Wiedza in Warsaw, Poland.

During the fifty years after WWII, I did not consider writing my memoirs. I did not have time to do this. Neither did I consider that my story would be of any importance and interest to anybody. And above all, I do believe that it would be more constructive to remember, rather, the good and positive incidents of my life and build the future on the basis of forgiveness, hoping that love will prevail.

However, in 1993, while visiting California, my wife and I stayed for few days in Los Angeles with our friends Michael and Danuta Zawadzki. Their son, Roman, listened to my story about what I had experienced in Auschwitz and told me outright, "This story needs be written down. I and 90 percent of people my age know but very little about these atrocities. If we heard anything at all, it was the tragedy of the Jewish Holocaust."

In 1994, I noticed an advertisement—or rather, a request—in a Polish newspaper. It was written by Mr. Louis A. Cavagnaro from Sun City, Arizona, and asking victims of Nazi terror to send him their accounts of persecution and suffering. I got in touch with him, and soon after becoming familiar with my experiences, he became the strongest advocate of my testimony. I was still hesitating how much I should write for Mr. Cavagnaro when, the following year, I went to see Father Eugene Ryan, the pastor of our Parish, to make arrangements for celebrating the golden jubilee of our marriage. Hearing that I met my wife just a few days after liberation from the concentration camp Bergen-Belsen, Father Ryan pressed me for more details of my past and then concluded, "This story must be written." Therefore, Roman Zawadzki, Louis Cavagnaro, and Father Ryan are to be credited for inspiring me to write this testimony.

To Mr. Cavagnaro, I owe particular gratitude for urging me to keep writing, but even more so for transferring my manuscript onto a computer diskette. Working with this diskette, Mr. Bogdan Grzybowski made necessary corrections and alternations while the final polishing was performed by Mr. Wladyslaw Poncet.

Thank you, fellows, for your effective and generous help.

And to you, dear reader, I have a simple request: when reading the following pages, take some time for thought and pray—not for me and those few who survived but for the thousands and thousands who did not.

Zbigniew M. Haszlakiewicz
December 18, 1996

CHAPTER I

Life in the General Government

For centuries, my family lived in the eastern territories of the Polish Commonwealth. They survived many disasters, wars, invasions, rebellions, and over one hundred years of methodical Russification efforts by the Russian czarist regime. After the First World War and after the Polish victory over Lenin's Red Army in 1920, only a part of these territories were included within the borders of the Republic of Poland. A modern Polish state was developing for nineteen years. Despite some friction between ethnic groups (Polish, Ukrainian, Jewish, Byelorussian, German, etc.), life in Poland was peaceful and pleasant compared to what was going on in those days in Germany and, in particular, across the eastern border—in the Soviet Union. The turmoil by both big neighbors of Poland was the prelude to an aggression. In September 1939, the Hakenkreuz from the west and the hammer and sickle from the east started rolling. Poland was over-run and occupied: the western half by Nazi Germany and the eastern half by Soviet Russia.

Within days, it became apparent that all Poles under Soviet occupation were doomed. All college graduates, teachers, police-men, government employees, and owners of shops and stores were deported to Siberia whereas rich persons; in particular, landowners and settlers (those who settled in Eastern Poland between 1920 and 1939) were exposed to mob law and often lynched on the spot.

At the age of ten, following the death of my parents in 1932, I went to live with my paternal uncle Henry, his wife Mary, and her mother. In September 1939, as the approaching Red Swarm got closer to our estate, we were attacked by a gang of hooligans inspired by the communists. After fighting them off with our weapons, it became apparent that we had no choice: we had to flee! Before loading the wagons and leaving our beautiful home, we were able to hide all our important documents. By not carrying documents, we were able to pretend to be refugees returning to the western part of Poland. After a month of tricky maneuvering, we crossed the demarcation line between Russian and German occupation. My uncle and aunt spoke fluent German, which helped us be tolerated by German patrols. However, soon it became apparent that the Germans of 1939 were a far cry from those they remembered from before the First World War.

The Nazi occupation of Poland, based on the exploitation of land and human resources, was brutal and ruthless. Western regions of Poland were annexed and incorporated into the Reich. With few exceptions, Poles were expelled from those territories. Those unable to work were sent to the so-called General Government (German name for not annexed but occupied Polish areas), and those fit for hard labor were sent to Germany. Expulsions were merciless. Police arrived without warning and forced people to leave their houses within ten to fifteen minutes. In the General Government proper, officers of the Polish Army were sought out particularly.

University professors were the first civilians to be imprisoned. Then so were many priests, teachers, and other intellectuals. Any person could be imprisoned for undetermined lengths of time for thousands of reasons or without any reason at all. For any disobedience or anti-German activity, people were shot on the spot. And not necessarily the guilty ones. Anyone who was on hand was shot just to scare the others and enforce obedience.

Mines, factories, farms, and forests were obligated to deliver to German authorities who demanded accounts of their products. Those quantities were established arbitrarily in theory as per German standards. Many producers did not make so much and could not deliver. These could expect any kind of punishment: confiscation of property, exile to Germany to do forced labor, imprisonment in a concentration camp, or a bullet. Extortion of goods from Polish producers became more sophisticated and effective when the quotas were set not for individuals but for entire communities. So for example, a rural village got an order to deliver within one year x tons of grain, y tons of potatoes, and z liters of milk, and a number of workers to be sent to Germany. Simultaneously, twenty of the most prominent persons in the village were singled out as hostages. When demanded quotas were not met, the hostages were sent to concentration camps. In the event of any kind of sabotage or anti-German violence in the village, these hostages were executed on the spot. Capital punishment was also applicable to Poles and their immediate families for helping Jews. When Germans found a Jew hidden in a house, they executed all inhabitants of that house. Therefore, it was more difficult to protect a Jewish fugitive in a larger multiunit building. For possession of a gun, you'd die, but for delivering arms to a Jewish ghetto, not only were you punished but also your family and your neighbors. For delivering food to the ghetto, people were sent to concentration camps.

Persons with Germanic names, after screening and confirming that they were not Jews, were told that they could join the *Herrenvolk* by signing a declaration that they were *Volksdeutsche* (i.e., of German extraction). Many privileges were available for such persons. However, if one did not sign such a declaration, he was persecuted and harassed.

Originally, our family name was preceded with the prefix Gottleb. It was written in all our documents. To avoid the invitation to the Volksdeutsche-hood, we decided to acquire new documents without that prefix. Simultaneously, in my new birth certificate, two years were added to my age to avoid being drafted into the youth labor battalions.

According to the plans of Hitler and his associates, all Poles were to be eliminated after using them as slaves in all kinds of German establishments. Consequently, there were no schools for Poles. Only four years of elementary education and some trade schools were allowed, no high schools or colleges. In fact, higher education was simply forbidden.

In the struggle for survival, the Polish nation organized not only an underground army, taking up outright fighting against both occupants, but also an underground school system. It was run by teachers, professors, and other individuals who hid their true identity and who did not get paid for this hard and dangerous work (except for gifts from grateful parents). Classes averaging seven or eight students were held in private quarters every day in a different one. Should the Germans capture such a class, everybody participating, together with the owners of the house, were taken by the Gestapo for investigation and subsequently sent to concentration camps. After escaping from the Soviets, my uncle, aunt (now my foster parents), and I lived for about four months in the small town of Przecław with a few other members of our family. Later, my foster parents received support from the bishop of Tarnów and moved to the small village of Siedliska, about fifteen miles south of Tarnów. I got a job (the first in my life) as an assistant forester in a forest near the city of Mielec. It was a relatively safe place to be in those days. In the fall of 1941, my uncle sent me a message that six miles south of their village, in the town of Cięszkowice, an underground high school had been organized, and he suggested that I take advantage of this opportunity. This I did and moved to live again with my foster parents while taking a daily train to Cięszkowice.

I had to complete my junior and senior terms of high school. This was accomplished within a year and a half, and in March 1943, at the age of 20, I passed the final examinations and graduated from the high school. Immediately thereafter, I became a "teacher" in our underground school because there was a considerable shortage of qualified instructors. From Siedliska, I would travel north to Tuchów and south to Gromnik and Cięszkowice to meet my pupils in someone's apartment and teach them history, math, and physics. At the same time, the underground army decided that since I had graduated, it would be necessary to prepare me for the eventual fight against the occupants. So I had to participate in various courses of military art. Therefore, in the spring of 1943, I was constantly traveling in a territory about fifteen miles long and three miles wide. To be prepared for a question about what I was doing there, I had registered my living quarters in Cięszkowice and obtained a document that said I was employed as a forester just north of Tuchów. Forester duties could be required during the day as well as at night. Thus, my presence on a road or in a train was always explainable.

Unfortunately, on June 19, 1943 at seven o'clock in the morning, I was headed to the railroad station in Tuchów in the company of two other young men. As we turned a corner, we ran into a sizeable detachment of SS troops. The encounter was very sudden, and we could not back out. One of my companions attempted to run and was shot dead by SS bullets.

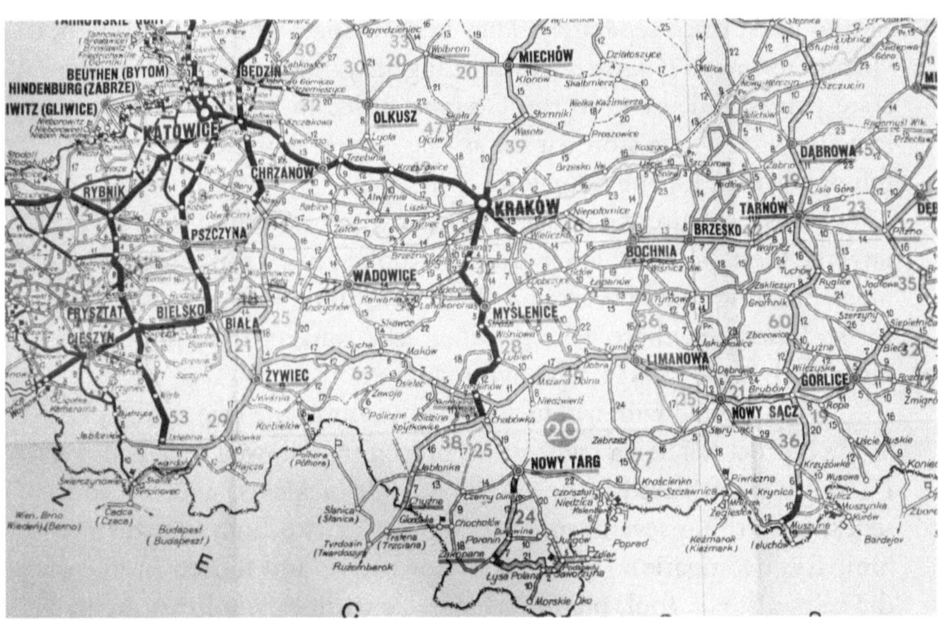

Chapter 2

In the Hands of the Gestapo

My friend Jurek Kuhn and I were apprehended immediately by the SS and questioned separately. They kept us apart while searching the vicinity for more *Banditen*. Not finding any, they loaded us into separate trucks and drove to the Gestapo office in Tarnów. I couldn't imagine what was in store for me as I sat, squeezed in between a truck full of SS men, for the hour-long trip.

I was not sure what the original use of the building was, but now the Gestapo occupied it. To me it looked like a four-story apartment building. On the ground floor were the interrogation offices. In the basement, there were prisoner cells, and on the upper floors most likely were the Gestapo living quarters.

I was greeted with a deluge of insults, hit in the face, and kicked in the buttocks. Then a registration procedure followed. Each answer I gave was considered to be a lie. I was hit or kicked and forced to repeat everything several times. After one or two hours of this preliminary investigation, I was taken downstairs and locked in one of the cells: a small, foul, pitch-dark cubicle without any furniture and without any hope. Severely beaten, I lay on the dirty floor, listening to the terrible screams and cries of other inmates. From time to time, the Gestapo men attempted to keep them quiet. They would open the door, shout and curse terribly, and beat the poor victim even more, sometimes to the extent that he stopped screaming forever. Then I prayed. I prayed to Almighty God for courage, for strength, and for inspiration on how to sustain myself for the coming interrogation without betraying the existence of our school, with seven teachers and sixty pupils. I prayed to deceive the Gestapo and avoid being physically or mentally incapacitated. And yes, I prayed for death instead of betrayal.

In the morning, after spending a ghastly night in that dungeon, they took me upstairs to one of the "offices." It was a large room with several windows facing the street, one door from the vestibule, and a second one in the corner, leading to a washroom. Facing this door at a distance of about twelve feet was a heavy wardrobe (possibly a safe). Facing the entry door, perhaps ten feet away, was a big solid desk with an armchair placed behind it. I noticed on top of this desk were a gun, a saber, two whips, and a folder with my name on the cover.

There were some scary tools hanging on the walls, but I did not have much time to study them. A guard pushed me in. Immediately an officer followed and took the seat behind the desk. His first question was, "Do you speak German?" My answer, "No," provoked the guard to kick me in the buttocks so that I almost fell on the desk. Instantly the officer grabbed the saber and, pointing it at my chest, pretended to defend himself. Then he laughed and said that for my sake, they will call some of the "charming" boys who spoke Polish.

With this, two more Gestapo men entered the room: one officer and one enlisted guard. The guard shouted to me in Polish, "You son of a bitch, we will count your bones in no time." However, the officer said in Polish: "Oh no, no, that will not be necessary if you talk to us like a reasonable human being." His language was perfect. Later he told me (with an oratory attempt to break my spirit by telling me that our cause had no chance against the might and wisdom of the Germans) that he studied Polish and literature at the University of Kraków.

He then started the interrogation and conducted it the whole time, occasionally translating certain things to the officer sitting behind the desk, who was making notes in a file. After a few harmless questions related to my personal data, he asked in a friendly manner, "Now tell us, please, what is the name of the organization you belong to?" I said that I did not belong to any organization. He said, "Don't lie. We know everything, and all you have to do is to confirm it and sign our report." I denied again that I belonged to any organization. Then all hell broke loose. All four of them pounced on me, hitting me with whatever they happened to have in their hands. I fell to the floor and was beaten and kicked some more by the four savages.

Suddenly the beating stopped. They lifted me up to my feet, sprayed my face with water, and started their juicy persuasive talk again. "We don't want to do you harm. Just admit that you are a member of NOW [Polish acronym for National Military Organization] and that you were working together with Jan Kruk so there will be no need for any more punishment for lying to us."

I did not admit to anything, and this caused another round of beating. At the end of the third beating session, one of them grabbed a gun, put it against my head, and said, "Tell us the truth, or I will shoot you like a dog." I said, "Please, do so!" That made them very angry. "Oh no! Not so easy, not so easy. First, you have to tell us everything you know! We will make you sing."

Upon that, they tied my hands behind my back with a chain and forced me to step up on a stool that they put in front of the second door. I had to stand with my back and tied hands against the door. Now they threw the substantial surplus of the chain over the door, and one of them started to pull on it. My tied hands were going up and up, and soon the terrible pain caused by the twist of my shoulders took over my entire consciousness.

It is not possible to describe the pain of forcibly twisted joints—in particular the shoulders. Within that pain, I could feel the muscles giving way, and I could hear the ligaments tearing. Then they kicked out the stool from under me. Everything tore apart in my shoulders. I hung, suspended by my hands, which were tied behind my back. Whoever reads these words should attempt to stretch your hands in that position; otherwise, you will not understand.

Even my torturers became silent for a while. Then one of them said, "Was this necessary? If you will tell us the truth, we will take you off this swing immediately." But I did not say anything. In fact, I could not say anything. The pain was so overwhelming, so cruel, and so unique. They let me hang like so for a while then asked their silly questions again. I did not answer. So they tied a rope to my legs and pulled me away from the door. They looped that rope over some hook on the safe and pulled me up. My body was now in a horizontal position some five or six feet above the floor, with legs tied to the safe and twisted hands to the door. I hung like this, facing the floor.

Now they brought two chairs, placing one on either side of my body. The two guards climbed upon these chairs, one with a whip and the other with a stick, and started to hit my back, buttocks, and legs. But those blows were not as painful as the still progressing tearing-apart of my shoulders. Soon the Polish-speaking officer approached with a knife in his hand and said, "Admit to the truth, or I will let the blood out of you." Then he stabbed me in the right side between the last rib and the belt. My blood started to flow, gathering in a puddle directly under me on the floor, and the Gestapo man said, "See, you stupid Polish patriot, how your blood is running. I presume it gives you the satisfaction that it runs for Poland, which is dead and will never rise again."

I was praying to lose consciousness, but it was not possible. The Gestapo soon tired and started to drink beer and smoke cigarettes as they sat at that big desk. And I was hanging like a hammock. Then their workday came to an end. They took me off that door and carried me to the cell in the basement. Apparently, it was already late in the evening when they brought me some soup. They put the bowl on the floor and locked the door. It was so dark that I could not see anything. My hands and arms were incapable of doing anything, so like an animal, I found the bowl by smell and slurped it up without the use of my hands.

This second night in the Gestapo basement was very painful. My entire body was aching and swelling. There was no position in which I could get that was comfortable. I wanted to cry and scream. However, my brain was working, and I reviewed in my mind the Gestapo's questions and intentions. It became clear to me that they did not know about the existence of our school; however, they considered me a member of the underground army. They obviously wanted to extricate out of me as much as possible on the subject of an underground military organization. This was bad for me personally because this charge carried the death penalty with it. However, it was good for the school and the people involved with it. So during that night, I decided to admit my membership in the underground army and direct Gestapo's attention to this particular activity so that my real involvement would remain hidden. Moreover, I really did not know any actual name and address of anybody from the underground military except those of two fellows who were with me at the time we ran into the SS detachment. So even in the worst circumstances, I could not give my oppressors any useful information.

The second day of interrogation started with only two officers present. The one who spoke Polish and the one in charge of the case, who, I was sure, understood Polish but spoke only German. After a lengthy talk by the Gestapo men trying to tell me that it made no sense not to admit that I was a member of the military organization, that they did not want to mistreat me but that I was forcing them to do so by my stubbornness, and that they knew anyhow who belonged to that organization. They quoted a few names, which could have really been underground-army organizers.

I asked them why they bothered to put all these questions to me when they knew everything. Then I told them that they would shoot me anyway if I admitted involvement with the Polish underground. To this they said that it was not a rule and that it was up to them to decide what to do with me. They offered me a cigarette, and when I could not hold it with my twisted hands, they said that they were sorry for my hands being in such a bad condition. Almost immediately thereafter, they hit me in the face for wasting their time by not saying what they expected me to say.

Finally, I admitted that I had been a member of the Polish underground army. They were very pleased and said that I should have done this yesterday. But now they started to press for details about the organization and people involved. Since I could not tell them much, they became angrier and angrier, and soon one of them started to hit me with the flat side of the saber. Then he grabbed one of my aching hands and started to twist it in a manner that caused terrible pain. Again he became very sweet and attempted to squeeze out information by persuasion in seemingly irrelevant conversation.

They asked me why my family moved to Siedliska then asked about my extended family: the Teodorowiczes and Kruszewskis in Tuchów and the Rozwadowskis in Gromnik. Then they asked why I moved to Cięszkowice when I had a job twenty kilometers north near Tuchów. When I said that I had done it because I had friends there who helped me get a room, they insisted that I tell them who those friends were. One of them was Jurek Kuhn, who was captured with me. The second was Mietek Podhorecki, in whose house I was rooming. I also had to mention Władek Ptak, J. Siebodzinski, and the Pagaczewski girls, with whom we were seen time and again by everybody in town. Terrible pressure was applied upon me to state that all or some of these people were also members of the military organization. I denied it categorically time and again, and I had to repeat the story about our friendships being casual and only platonic.

All I could admit to was that I knew only the two men captured with me and one more, who was killed a couple of months earlier, and that all we did was learn military rules from the book, preparing ourselves to fight against the Soviet Army in case it defeated the Germans. This caused them to call in the guard, and they threatened to hang me on the door again. Since I didn't say anything else, they did just that, and the terror of yesterday repeated itself but with more excruciating pain. This time I fell unconscious and only regained the ability to think when I found myself back in the basement dungeon.

My body was a wreck. My arms were out of control completely, and my hands were swollen and stiff. My legs were stretched out of their joints. In particular, my knees were weak and insecure. My entire back was a bloody mess, and my face swollen and blue. Two teeth were missing. Everything was in pain.

On the morning of the third day, two guards came, poured some water on my face, and let me drink it. They also brought coffee and a piece of bread, but I could not lift it to my mouth. One of the guards held the bread so that I could take two or three bites, then they helped me to three sips of coffee. After this "breakfast," they ordered me to go again to the office. But I could not walk, especially up the stairs, so the guards helped me. This help was rough and caused much pain, but without it, I would not have made it to that terrible office. There, surprisingly, they provided a chair for me. I was sitting in front of the officer behind the desk. There was also a civilian interpreter standing nearby. The officer was reading from his notes the digest of my so-called confession. I attempted to protest whenever he mentioned the criminal or sabotage activities of our organization. But he, always in such cases, grabbed a whip and shouted for me to keep quiet. After the review of these notes, the officer said that they (Gestapo) would verify the truth of my testimony and type up the report, which I would have to sign. But if they found out that I lied about something, they would interrogate me again. Then he pulled out a list of names and told me to say yes if I knew the person whose name he read.

There were about twenty names on that list, most unknown to me, but there were a few relatives and a few colleagues from our illegal school. Each time I said yes, he ordered me to explain in detail what kind of relationship or association I had with that person. After finishing all these inquisitive questions, they left me alone in this macabre "office." An hour or more passed when guards burst in and ordered me out. I attempted to get up, but my bottom was glued to the chair by sweat, blood, and pus. The Gestapo men laughed, spewed a few vulgar remarks, then detached me from the chair and helped me go out into the corridor. There were other mutilated prisoners waiting. Those in better physical condition were ordered to help me walk to the police van that took us to the prison. Those three days were the worst in my life. Everything that happened thereafter was horrible, harsh, and difficult to survive but never so painful, so devastating, for body and soul.

Members of the Geheime Staatspolizei (Gestapo) were the worst people living in this world—so cruel, so ruthless, so perfidious, and double-dealing. No other Nazi organization was so efficient in subduing millions of Europeans to their rule. And their terror also included other Germans. However, half a century later, I wonder how many of them were ever brought to justice.

Gestapo H.Q. in Tarnów

Prison in Tarnów

(Photos taken in 1995)

CHAPTER 3

Prison in Tarnów

There was no concentration camp in Tarnów; however, there was a sizeable prison. Polish authorities built it just a few years before WWII. It was a building of five levels with the floor plan in the shape of the capital letter *E*. Prison cells were on both sides of the corridor in each of the projecting wings, which were called A, B, and C. The interconnecting building had a corridor running the length on one side and rooms facing the street on the other. In this building, on the ground floor, there were reception and administrative offices. I think that on the upper floor, there were women's cells whereas the basement (which was only partially underground) contained the kitchen and storage facilities.

The basement was called level 1. The floor, about 1.5 meters above ground, was level 2. The upper floors were 3, 4, and 5. The structure was reinforced concrete. On level 1, the floors, walls, and ceilings were of exposed and painted concrete. On the upper floors, the walls and ceilings were plastered and painted white (originally), whereas some kind of artificial material covered the concrete floor. It was of a softwood-like texture and very smooth. On level 2, the floor covering was black while on the upper levels, it was red. Windows in the cells were about 75 square centimeters (two feet, six inches) except on level 1, where different sizes were used depending on the purpose of the room. The windows, of course, were secured with heavy iron bars and glazed sashes, which projected inward. Their spacing, I believe, was 2 meters (six feet, seven inches) on-center. So if a 25-centimeter (ten-inch) wall was built between these windows, it provided a room 1.75 meters (five feet, nine inches) wide. Since all rooms were about 4.5 meters (fourteen feet, nine inches) deep, a cell for one prisoner had approximately 8 square meters (85 square feet) of floor area. Cells with two windows were originally intended for four prisoners. In the corner of each cell was a flush water closet, which was also considered to be a wash basin and the only source of drinking water. (This was a luxury compared to older prisons, where a portable container served as a latrine, whereas water, if any, was held in a bucket.) In each small cell there were the following: one bed (with a bag filled with straw as a mattress), one chair, and one table. In the larger cells were four such sets of furnishings—one for each of the four intended prisoners. All were of steel, attached to the walls, and collapsible. If all this furniture was in a raised position, the room was free of any obstruction. In the ironclad doors were peepholes, through which one could look in from the outside only. Below the peephole was a little door that could be opened to shout some order without opening the door proper.

The prison was designed for some four to five hundred inmates. The Germans, however, squeezed in up to two thousand prisoners. Thus, in a single cell were four or five prisoners, and in those designed for four, there were up to twenty. The prison was managed by four or five Germans, all old professional wardens, and staffed by a number of prewar Polish guards. However, sentries outside the building were German Security Police. The duty of the Polish guards was to maintain order inside the building, supervise the preparation and distribution of food, guide prisoners to and from the cells, and guard criminal inmates, who worked in prison workshops or sometimes outside the prison. Political prisoners were not allowed to work or perform any duties; this was to prevent the possibility of contact with the outside world and any attempts to escape.

It was a short ride from the Gestapo headquarters to the prison. I believe we were eight prisoners in the van. All were badly mistreated, but I think that I was in the worst shape. We arrived at the reception room of the prison and were quickly registered in their books and files. We had to deposit all our belongings except the suits we were wearing and a handkerchief. I did not have much to deposit, only my empty wallet since all my documents were removed already by the Gestapo, and I didn't have much money in it to begin with.

One of the German wardens was reviewing our transmittal documents, which were issued by the Gestapo, and ordered one of the Polish guardsmen to take me to the room A.IV.10. That meant wing A, fourth level, room 10. It was a single cell, and I was alone. This was good and bad. To my advantage, it was a quiet place where I could rest in relative comfort because I had the bed all to myself. There were some disadvantages, however. Above all, there was the fear that the Gestapo had not given up on me yet and wanted to keep me in isolation until further notice. And, of course, there was the terrible problem of my condition. I could do nothing with my arms, which by now resembled two pendulums with big red-and-blue balls hanging on strings of bones covered by skin. Fortunately, I did not need to unbutton my pants since, for the last three days, I didn't eat much either. Virtually nothing. I asked the guard to give me some water to drink, but he just said that it was not permitted for them to listen or talk to prisoners. Then he left, locking the door. Leaning against the wall, I lowered myself to my knees and said a prayer, thanking the Lord for letting me survive this long and asking for more strength to keep me going on further. Then I laid myself down on my stomach on the floor and fell asleep.

In Tarnów prison, the worst for the prisoners was the incessant hunger. So-called food given to the inmates by the prison administration consisted of the following: in the morning, a piece of bread three by three by one-half inches (7.5 centimeters × 7.5 centimeters × 1.25 centimeters) in size and one-half liter of black warm water called coffee and in the late afternoon, one liter of greenish liquid called soup. The green color was from the stalks of sunflowers cooked in water. Perhaps in other times of the year, there were other ingredients used to transform water into soup. In the summer, it was sunflower or something similar. Anyway, on such a diet, people could not survive long, and it was well known in Southern Poland that the mortality rate in Tarnów prison was high.

Fortunately, in a rare humanitarian impulse, at some point in 1942, German authorities in the General Government permitted a Polish charitable organization to be established. It was called RGO (Rada Główna Opiekuńcza, or Main Charitable Council). Among many other charitable activities, RGO collected food throughout the country and then distributed it to the needy. In the summer of 1943, when I was in Tarnów prison, the food that we received from RGO exceeded in nutritional value three times the prison rations. It arrived in the form of bread and soup. Every second day, RGO food was distributed, alternating between bread and soup each day.

On the day of my arrival, it was the bread distribution. I woke up at the squeak of the opening door. The same Polish guard who brought me to my cell held the door open, and two criminal inmates pulled a blanket loaded with pieces of bread, each roughly one kilogram (2.2 pounds) in weight but of different shapes and color. That was because the bread was collected from a village where people dropped into the basket what they had, and it was all home baked.

One piece was thrown into my cell. However, the guard, seeing that I was struggling to get up from the floor without the use of my hands, stepped in, picked up the bread, and put it on the metal table projecting out of the wall. Then he ordered one of the criminals to bring a cup of water and another to help me get up and sit down on the metal seat, which was also projecting out of the wall next to the table. I sat on my thighs because it was less painful. When the first criminal arrived with the water, he was ordered to help me drink some of it. Oh, what a relief it was! Then he put the cup full of water on the table next to the bread. But the guard took another look at my hands, shrugged his shoulders, shook his head, and said to the criminals, "He needs a straw." They hurriedly left my cell, locked the door, and proceeded with the distribution of bread to the other prisoners.

More than half an hour later, my door opened again, and one of the criminals ran in and put a piece of natural straw into my cup. None of them spoke a word to me. But their help was so essential. Now I had bread and water—the best meal of my life. I have no words to describe how tasty it was. I ate that bread by biting off piece after piece. I was not yet finished when the guard let in one of the inmates who lowered my bed.

I ate that bread piece by piece until the entire kilogram was gone. I drank my water and lay on the bed, on my stomach, to avoid hurting my back. I slept for twelve hours until they woke me up, bringing "breakfast" and ordering the bed up. Yes, this was the prison rule. During the daytime, all beds must be lifted up and locked to the walls. No sleeping during the daytime! I had to be helped to handle the bed, and the official micro piece of bread and the coffee had been arranged so that I could reach them without using my hands.

Later that day, they took me to the shower. I was terribly dirty and stank, and my clothes were good for nothing. In fact, the sleeves of my jacket and shirt had to be torn in half because they could not be pulled over my swollen hands. Under the guard's supervision, one of the criminal inmates took my clothing off me and, after the shower, helped pull on me some pants (not mine) and a sleeveless shirt. I also got back my shoes and my belt. All this was done in a hurry and without a word being spoken. Then they took me back to my cell and left without paying any special attention to me for the next two days.

Three full days after my arrival at the prison, a Gestapo order that kept me isolated apparently lifted, and what was even more important was that my family learned of my whereabouts. Luckily for about 1 or 2 percent of the prisoners in Tarnów prison, the Polish guards that were retained on their job by the Germans did cooperate with the Polish underground. They served as intermediaries between the prisoners and the outside world. Maybe not all of them and maybe not for patriotic duty but for profit, but nevertheless, they risked their freedom and lives to carry messages out from the prisoners and bring in food and medicines. For security reasons, they served only those individuals who were known to the underground authorities as trustworthy and reliable. They also demanded extremely high compensation. Since a vast majority of the prisoners didn't have anything to do with the underground movement, the number of those taken care of was limited.

Thus, after three nights in cell A.IV.10, I was transferred to the cell C.II.15. This was accomplished with a lot of shouting, swearing, and rushing. My new cell was a two-window chamber (i.e., with four iron beds). But I joined a crowd of eleven—the inhabitants of this cell, so together we were twelve. No wonder I was greeted by fellow cellmates without enthusiasm. However, within minutes, their attitude had changed. When they noticed the condition of my body and heard that the Gestapo caused it, almost everybody in the room wanted to help me. The senior in the cell was Mr. Pokorny. There were two or three older men in the room, but he had already been in that prison for almost two years. That was extremely unusual since every three or four months, when the number of prisoners in the building exceeded 1,500, the Germans shipped the entire contents of the prison to a concentration camp (in most cases, to Auschwitz), leaving only a few ordinary (criminal) inmates and those singled out by the Gestapo or other German authorities.

Mr. Pokorny's case apparently was not yet closed, so he survived five such evacuations of the prison. He was a teacher and, in fact, a principal of the primary public school in the town of Zakliczyn. What his "crime" was, I did not know. It was not wise to discuss such matters when an investigation was still in progress. He was about forty years old, knowledgeable, very gentle, and a good man. Thanks to him, I recovered almost completely from these injuries caused by the Gestapo and gained spiritual strength as well, which was so much needed for the ordeal to come.

After a brief inspection of my face, back, and hands, he exclaimed, "Those bastards have really fixed up this boy." Then, turning to the cellmates, he said, "Gentlemen, we have to save this young soul." And sure enough, a most convenient spot for sleeping was assigned to me. Turns were established as to who was supposed to take care of my bed, who would feed me, and who would help at the latrine and with washing.

Mr. Pokorny himself said, "I will take care of his body." And from the next morning it started: massages and exercise, a few minutes of rest, and again massages and exercise happened hour after painstaking hour but poised me for success. To make massaging possible and more effective, some ointment had been smuggled in together with another medicine used to heal my external wounds.

I am certain that Mr. and Mrs. Kuhn, parents of my friend Jurek, who was captured with me, had provided these medicines. The Kuhns were pharmacists and operated two prescription drugstores—one in Kraków and one in Cięszkowice. Unfortunately, their own son had been beaten by the Gestapo in a different manner than I. His hands and legs were less damaged; however, his internal organs were injured somehow. In particular, his liver was displaced, and he was bleeding internally and only semiconscious. When they brought him to the prison, Jurek's condition was so critical they took him directly to the prison hospital on the fifth level. Nobody knew how much money it cost. Nevertheless, the Kuhns succeeded in gaining permission to send a specialist to treat their son. His help and a multitude of medicines saved Jurek's life. During the entire three months that I spent in Tarnów prison, Jurek remained under special care in the hospital. In the meantime, my rehabilitation was progressing. First, I gained control of two fingers in my right hand, and then it became possible to lift up my left forearm just a bit. Then after a few days of training, I succeeded to hook my right hand by the left one and move it to an appropriate position, and now with three fingers working, I unbuttoned my pants. For this I got a big hurrah from my cellmates. It soon became necessary to learn how to hold a spoon, take some soup on it, hold it steady, and bow my body to gulp that soup—the second hurrah! Mr. Pokorny kept massaging and inventing new exercises. Besides carefully improving movements of my hands, I had to walk, do knee bends, bend my body in all directions, etc. Mr. Pokorny held this drill systematically. Soon other prisoners joined me, and an entire exercising class developed.

As the next step in regaining control over my hands, there were some very funny attempts to hunt flies. A flyswatter was made from an old shoe sole on a stick. I had to hit a fly sitting on a table or on the wall. It took a million tries before I succeeded—another hurrah. The mood in our cell was rather good because soon it became clear that this was one of the lucky places where the inhabitants were under the special care of the Polish prison guards. Every day, at least one or two of us got grub (i.e., some food supplied by his family or the underground organization and smuggled into the prison by a guard). Delivering it into the cell was a tricky procedure. The most common way was to sneak it in when regular prison meals were being distributed. At such times, the door was opened by a guard who, in most instances, pretended to be nasty, swearing and rushing us to pick up our rations. When the package was small and he could hide it within his uniform, he would place himself so that the door, which he held by one hand, was hiding the front or the side of his body. Then, with the second hand, he would quickly remove the package and throw it into our room. More common, however, was that the package was carried by one of the criminal inmates who were actually distributing official food. Usually, there were three of them. Two were carrying a big container with the coffee, and the third one a tray with slices of bread. When soup was served, two carried the container, and the third would ladle the soup into our bowls.

The criminal prisoner's dress in Tarnów was loose white paja-malike suits, so it was easy to hide a relatively large package under it. When delivering a package, they placed their container very close to our door, then a commotion was created, during which one of the carriers sneaked into our cell and dropped the package. Of course, there were other opportunities to pass on those illegal food parcels— for instance, when bringing us back from a walk in the prison court or from the shower or when the legal (permitted) parcels sent by the families were distributed.

Yes, we could get packages from home, but clothing only. And once every two weeks, we could also send our laundry back home. The so-called distribution of these laundry parcels was a particular ceremony. I do not know if this was a daily routine or a weekly one, but it happened usually in the afternoon. Prisoners for whom something arrived were called into the main corridor on the second level near the main entrance, where it was extra wide. One German warden, two Polish guards, and a few "criminals" would stand at a table. In your presence, your parcel was cut open by one of the guards, and the contents dumped on the table. The German would watch carefully while the two guards would remove the contents piece by piece, shake them, check each pocket, and unfold each fold. Sometimes the warden ordered to tear something open. Sometimes he inspected a piece with his own fingers. And usually, they found articles that were not permitted for prisoners. Those would be letters, money, anything made of metal, books, pictures, playing cards, and, of course, any kind of food.

Almost nobody could refrain from the temptation to hide something not permitted. Eventually, the prisoner would get only his shirts or a handkerchief whereas everything else was confiscated and dumped into separate piles. Food would be taken to the kitchen, intended as ingredients for our daily soup. Books, letters, and pictures were sent away for destruction. Metals were to be sent to armament-making factories. Only money was scrupulously added to the prisoner's account.

However, our illegal packages, delivered by the Polish guardsmen, contained everything that was prohibited.

One month after my arrival to Mr. Pokorny's cell, I was in relatively good physical shape except that the control over my hands was not reliable. It was then that I was again summoned by the Gestapo. This was very scary news, but there was no choice. I was taken there in a police van similar to the one that brought me to the prison. I was back in the same room with the same officer and the same interpreter. Fortunately, this time they hardly asked me any questions. They read to me their report of the investigation including my so-called confession and ordered me to sign it. However, when I attempted to do that, my hand did not work properly, so my signature was nothing but zigzags. When the Gestapo man noticed this, he said with considerable cynicism, "I see your hands are improving. This is good. We will need them! Even though you deserve the death penalty for your crimes against the Deutsche Reich, our great *Führer* decided to let you pay for those crimes by working for us for as long as it will be necessary. Should you not work where we will send you, we will then send you this." And he pulled out his gun and pointed it at me.

I went back to my prison cell, feeling relieved that most likely I would not see the Gestapo again. In the meantime, I learned that soon after our arrest, German Security Police staged several raids on

Tuchów, Gromnik, and Cięszkowice. They questioned members of my family and the Kuhn family on the spot, and they arrested Władek Ptak and Stan Pagaczewski, the brother of one of our girlfriends. Pagaczewski had a weak body and was an absentminded astronomer. Two or three weeks after his arrest, they let him go home. However, Władek Ptak had been jailed for good.

All such news as well as all important world news were spread about the prison via sign language from wing to wing or by Morse code within a wing. Some of this news originated in the hospital on the fifth level (where specialists were employed) and from workshops on the first level (where nonpolitical prisoners were working).

I am writing these memories fifty-two years after the events described herein took place. Therefore, I do not remember all the details. In particular, names—with few exceptions—escape my memory. For example, from the eleven fellows whom I shared the cell with, I remember only the last name of Mr. Pokorny; I am not sure of his first name (Eugene or Edward). Another one was called Pan Stanisław (Mr. Stanley), who at home was a *sołtys* (i.e., a peasant village elder; in more modern terms, an elected village administrator), remains in my memory only under his first name. But I remember that he was from a village near the town of Bochnia and was imprisoned as one of the hostages because his village was short two or three tons of grain in obligatory contribution to occupation authorities. Since it was a small fraction of the required contribution and the people had promised that they would deliver that grain, the Germans took him to be in prison only until the delivery would be accomplished.

Six of my cellmates were simply taken in a raid on a residential community of Tarnów, arrested in their homes without any explanation why. One was the victim of a police dog at a railroad station when his satchel was discovered to have meat in it. This was a common occurrence in those days—that city people would go into the country to exchange their belongings for food. This was *verboten*, so the man was put into jail. Two fellows in my cell did not say a word about where they were from and why they shared our predicament. I strongly suspect that at least one of them was a Jew who was captured accidentally outside the ghetto and, fortunately, was not recognized as such.

It is significant that of the twelve men in this cell, only two were subject to careful investigation by the security authorities, who also decided our guilt and penalty. This meant there was no court of law and no defense; just the arbitrary whim of a few bloodthirsty policemen would decide our human fate. No wonder! Let's consider how many security and judicial personnel the Nazi regime would have to employ if they would extend to everyone as much time as they did to me. It took roughly three Gestapo men three days, which means nine days per one security agent. Since everyday twenty new prisoners were delivered to Tarnów prison, it would be necessary for them to have 180 Gestapo agents in Tarnów alone. That was ten times as many as they could afford. But the purpose of all these arrests was not German security but to lock up and eliminate as many Poles as possible.

Our cell windows faced a prison maintenance yard where all kinds of activities took place—delivery of raw food or fuel, garbage pickup, drying laundry, and refilling mattresses with straw, for example. For a few days in August, they even brought in machinery to thrash grain hauled in from the prison farm.

About two months after my imprisonment, a dreadful incident involving our cell took place. One afternoon, our Mr. Stanley was standing on an illegally placed bed, looking out the window. He spotted a criminal sweeping the yard. He called him and negotiated a purchase of cigarettes. He was told to drop the money first followed by a string to pull up the pack of cigarettes. This was the usual procedure, but this time all hell broke loose.

Terrible shouts in German—"Halt! Halt! *Bleibt stehen!*"—were directed at the poor criminal and our Mr. Stanley. Soon two guards appeared and were ordered by the German warden, who was standing with his gun ready in the window of level 1, just below our window, to "grab the criminal and the paper he attempted to pick up from the pavement." The warden had been standing in his window, unnoticed, during the conversation between the criminal and Mr. Stanley.

Within minutes, two German and several Polish guards were in our cell. They chased us out of the room and proceeded with an ultrathorough search of our den. They came out with bags full of illegal items. This was a terrible mishap. Our cell was emptied of everything moveable, and we were locked back in. It took about an hour for the chief warden, who was outside of the prison at that time, to arrive and begin a careful investigation. This hour gave us time to invent some kind of strategy, how to defend ourselves, and, above all, how to hide the entire chain of conspirators helping us.

After a quick analysis of the situation, we decided that only three of us would admit that the illegal things were ours. The rest would swear that they were innocent. The selection of two culprits was simple. Mr. Pokorny volunteered as the one who collected all knives, spoons, books, playing cards, etc. when he was transferred from one cell to another many times during his long stay in the prison. Mr. Stanley declared that he was the owner of all the money (which was smuggled in a month ago after being sewn into his heavy Uplander pants) and that all cigarettes and matches were his, purchased through the window from various people working in the yard. The third volunteer had to become the owner of the food. This was the most difficult to explain—how we got it without help by someone. Since no one was eager to take this burden and the silence extended for a few minutes, I decided to volunteer. It occurred to me that I could take advantage of the grain-thrashing incident, which took place just a few days before.

When we were taken to the reception hall, now converted into a courtroom, the situation looked bleak. All four wardens and a few policemen were present—all Germans, some of them speaking Polish. Fortunately, I did not notice any Gestapo or SS men. The Polish prison guards were not present. We were each called in separately. Pointing to the pile of goods found in our cell, they asked, "From where did you get it?"

When my turn came, I answered that not everything was mine. "So what's yours?" they asked. I pointed to a sizeable piece of bread, one half of a chicken, a small can of fat, and two apples. That made them very excited and caused a barrage of questions: "How did you get it?" "Who delivered this?" "When?" etc. So I told them that I stole a package that was being pulled up by a string dropped from one of the upper floors during the evening when the grain-thrashing was taking place. This astounded them. Some shouted, "Lie! Lie! That's impossible!" but the chief warden said that I should be held separately for further questioning after listening to what the other culprits had to say. After about one hour, only three of us remained, separated, in the corridor adjacent to the reception hall. Then they called me in again and started the questioning over again. In the crossfire of questions, I had to be careful to stick to my story, which was as follows:

"The grain-trashing was going on day and night. It was noisy, so I could not sleep. It was also very hot, so we kept the windows open despite the noise. I was standing on my bed, looking out the window, and watching a crowd of 'criminals' working on and around the threshing machine. This was about two windows away to my left. All of a sudden, I noticed a rope spanning my window, stretching diagonally higher on my left, lower on my right. Then it became tight and slowly started moving up and left from my vantage point. In a short time, a sizeable package wrapped in a fiber bag was in front of my window. Impulsively I grabbed it. It was too big to fit between the window bars, so I called Mr. Stanley to help me. He got a knife from Mr. Pokorny and quickly cut the upper and lower rope, which was violently jerking in an attempt to pull the package out of my hands. Then we cut the bag and removed the contents piece by piece."

For half an hour, the Germans attempted to confuse me and distract me from my version. Then they ordered me out of the room and called on Mr. Stanley. Thankfully, he confirmed having helped me get the contents of the package through the window. And that was the end of the interrogation. After a while, all three of us were called into the "courtroom." I was surprised to notice that all four of our wardens were now in a jovial and relieved mood as compared to what it was one or two hours before.

Some of the German policemen were glaring at us with hate but also with noticeable respect. The chief warden became very serious and told us that we had violated many rules of his prison and that this extremely serious matter deserved the maximum penalty within his jurisdiction, and therefore, we would be locked in a penalty cell for fifteen and half days. This, in normal circumstances, was equal to a death sentence because you only got a mini slice of bread and one cup of water daily. Even for a prisoner who, for months, already was on the prison diet, this was not enough for survival.

I was told that within the last three years, only a few survived seven days in the penalty cell, and only one made it to the fourteenth day. It was a single cell in the A wing on level 1 (i.e., halfway underground with a window half the size of a normal one and located way up at the ceiling). There was no bed, no table, and no chair. The walls and floor of rough concrete were unpainted and with visible moisture. There was no water closet, only a latrine bucket. However, there were certain circumstances to our advantage. First of all, the entire prison was already filled up to its capacity, even by Nazi standards. Conventional prisoners occupied a few of these penalty cells, and a few more by other penalized inmates. And there was a rule in this prison that in one cell, there could only be one prisoner, three, or more, never two! Therefore, all three of us were locked in one cell at the far end of the corridor.

Most important, however, for us was the indebtedness of all the Polish guards and of the "criminal" helpers involved, who we did not betray. We felt them relax in their behavior immediately after the verdict of the chief warden was announced and the Germans led us to the penalty corridor. On this corridor, one German was always present whenever the door to a cell was opened. On the other corridors, most of the time, the Polish guards performed all the functions alone without German supervision.

It was evening, perhaps seven or eight o'clock, when we were locked in our new "quarters." For the next twenty hours, the door was not opened. That was a tough twenty hours. We did not sleep at all since it was not only inconvenient but also dangerous to sleep on the bare, wet concrete. We were hungry and exhausted yet happy that our fatal mishap did not turn into a bigger disaster.

After thoroughly discussing the entire incident, we arrived at the conclusion that our German wardens really did not want to overemphasize this case. Who knows why? Were they afraid that their higher authorities would consider them responsible for allowing such a disorder in their prison? Or were they normal professional bureaucrats who do not like any commotion and change in their daily routine? Or were they taking bribes themselves? It was difficult to attribute any "humanitarian" reason for the soft handling of our case since so many of their "lodgers" were starving of hunger, enduring miserable conditions, and, worst of all, subjected to raids by mad (usually drunk) members of the Gestapo, SS, and other Nazi thugs assigned to terrorize occupied territories (during such raids, prisoners would be pulled out of the cells and shot for fun). Anyway, they accepted our stories as believable, wrote appropriate reports, and closed the case quickly. All well and good, but how were we going to survive these fifteen days?

At 6:00 p.m. the next day, our door suddenly opened. One warden, a guard, and two "criminals" appeared. The criminals, under the supervision of the guard, took away the latrine bucket to be emptied (usually, this should have been done by cell inhabitants themselves, but those serving penalty were not allowed to leave their cell under any circumstances).

In the meantime, the warden was shouting German obscenities at us and told us how bad we were and that we deserved nothing but starvation in this cell. Then, however, he said the chief warden was a very good man and had ordered to provide us with mattresses, which would be given for nights only. Our bucket was brought back. When they were putting the bucket in the corner of the room, one criminal said to the other one, "Before you pee, look!" Then they brought in three boards, each five feet long and twenty inches wide, and said, "Here are your mattresses," at which the German shouted, "No talking!" and locked the door.

Mr. Pokorny said, "Do you remember what that guy said? Let's take a look." He lifted the cover on the bucket, and sure enough, inside were three pieces of bread wrapped in cement-bag paper. From then on, every morning at 6:00 a.m. they took away our boards and furnished our official rations of one slice of bread and one cup of water. At 6:00 p.m. they pushed in our boards. Every day they also invented another trick to smuggle in some extra food. The food smuggled into our penalty cell was, in most instances, what was confiscated from the incoming clothing parcels and, as such, was extremely high in all kinds of nutrients because the families of the prisoners, hoping their kin would get that piece of food, prepared it to give him the most in the smallest piece.

On the sixth day of our "isolation," a miracle happened. Mr. Stanley was released from the prison. It happened so suddenly and unexpectedly that we could not give him the addresses of our families. He was gone, and a problem developed. We two could not remain in the cell alone. Soon thereafter we got a third fellow. Again, I do not remember his name, but I remember his appearance and discussions with him. He was a communist activist. It was the first time in my life that I had an occasion to talk to a communist, and this one was a determined ideologist. He was very eloquent, and for the entire two days that he was with us, he attempted to convince us how beautiful it would be when there would be no religion, no other political parties, and no frontiers between nations; when everything would be common property; when all services would be free; and when people would work no more than four days a week.

He was tedious with his fanaticism, but worse, his presence in our cell prevented our illegal food supply from coming through. After he left (his penalty was a short one for arguing with the guard), they took Mr. Pokorny to another cell, and for the remaining days of my penalty, I was alone. It was extremely boring and disturbing to be alone in such a confinement without even the possibility of sitting down. The feeling of hopelessness was oppressing. And since I was now supplied well with water and all kinds of fancy foods, I was gaining weight, so much so that the guards spread the news that I was swollen from hunger.

In the last two or three weeks in Tarnów, I was locked again together with Mr. Pokorny and three other fellows in a single cell on the C.II. corridor. It was a former guard's room that was now used as a cell. There was no iron furniture attached to the walls, nor was there a water closet. But this was to our advantage. We had to pile up our straw mattresses so that during the day, at least two of us could lie down on the pile. We had to take our latrine bucket out to the toilet across the corridor, and this was the most convenient time to smuggle in our illegal food rations. Every morning, we would conduct a hunt for bedbugs. Each of my four cellmates had an assigned territory on the walls and on the ceiling. My duty was to lie down on the pile of mattresses and observe the entire room. When I spotted a bedbug, I called to action the fellow in whose territory the bug was located. In the very early part of the mornings, we would be busy catching a hundred bedbugs or more.

By the end of September, the time had come to vacate the prison. For several days, corridor after corridor, prisoners were taken downstairs to the showers and weighed as well. I do remember my weight: 159 pounds. Then our belongings, which were kept in the warden's storage, were returned to us. Mine included the new suit sent to me by my foster parents. We signed some papers, which later were given to our escorts.

A few days later, on a normally quiet prison morning, a terrible commotion woke us up. The noise of hundreds of boots, many doors being noisily opened, and, above all, shouts of "*Raus! Raus!*" alarmed us and almost caused a panic. In anticipation of such a beginning to our journey, we slept in our clothes and with our bags (if any) at hand, ready. Our corridor was filled with SS men who were shouting, pushing, and kicking. We were chased down the stairs to the prison yard and packed like sardines into the military trucks that delivered us to the railroad station.

Chapter 4

On the Road to Auschwitz

A long train of about twenty boxcars was waiting for us along a side ramp of the Tarnów RR depot. The ramp and train were surrounded by hundreds of SS, some of them with dogs. We were unloaded from the trucks at one end of the ramp and had to run along the train to the furthest empty car. The SS men followed us and, at times, set their dogs on us. Then they lined us up in five long, parallel rows. They counted groups of fifteen to twenty of us (by fives; seventy-five to one hundred men), and we were assigned to the cars. Two or three SS men were assigned to each group, and they were the ones who hastened us into the cars. Inside, they ordered us to sit down on the floor. The first five had to sit down with their backs against the rear wall of the car and with their legs spread out; the next five had to sit down between the legs of the first row, with their backs against the chests of those behind; and so on, row by row until the legs of the last row hit the front wall of the car.

Such a boxcar had a sliding door in the center of its side wall. At this door, a space of about nine feet long and three feet deep was kept free of prisoners, and two SS men sat there on small stools, facing each other so that one was watching half of the car, which was behind the back of the other one. Most of the time they kept this door open, for this was the only source of light and fresh air. The SS men were extremely tense and attentive, apparently believing that they were guarding a carload of dangerous "Banditen." There was a third SS man sitting or standing on the top of the car. Every hour or two, they would change positions. During each change, they inspected the car bottom and all around. All these precautions were in anticipation that some of us would attempt to escape. However, they were also afraid of a potential attack by the underground army. It has already happened that the underground people liberated their VIPs, who were transported by German authorities.

Unfortunately, nobody liberated us. Our train was rolling and stopping, rolling and stopping. In fact, there was more standing than rolling. And we were sitting always in the same position with no food, no drink, and no latrine. This was a terrible problem for many. To be hungry and thirsty is one thing, but having no possibility of relieving oneself was a particular torture. Some people could not hold. The stench in our car became unbearable.

The guards threatened that they would shoot all those dirty pigs on the spot. But under the circumstances, they could not identify who was the culprit, and despite the threat, more and more prisoners were screaming that they couldn't control themselves anymore. This was a natural necessity. And despite sitting next to the open door, the guards were also exposed to the stinking air inside the car. The situation was alike in all the cars. So finally, the train stopped in an open field. The SS escort formed a tight circle surrounding a narrow area on one side of our train and let us out.

Grotesque, dramatic, and tragic was the view of 1,700 men relieving themselves in a hurry next to each other on this narrow strip of land, some of them desperately attempting to clean their dirty pants with sand. It is hard to describe this display of savagery, shame, and humiliation of people in such circumstances. It was my first lesson of mass dehumanization.

It was sixty miles from Tarnów to Kraków, but it took our train ten to twelve hours. When we arrived in Kraków, it was already dark, and nobody paid much attention. So the train stood on a side rail track until the morning. We sat in the same order and in the same position we had assumed in Tarnów. Whoever fell asleep would lean against a neighbor—the one behind, the one in front, or the one on either side. Only those sitting along the walls could have leaned against the wallboards.

The SS guards left the car and locked the door, so it was dark, stinky, and very uncomfortable. The absence of guards permitted us to move. Some of us stood up, but it was impossible to get anywhere. We wanted everybody to get up; this would have made it possible to move around a bit. But many were already so exhausted that they didn't want to change their position whatsoever. Thus, we had to sit down again.

When we were not guarded, there was a lot of talking among ourselves. The topic of most of these conversations was "Where are we going?" The Germans did not tell us, but the prevailing opinion was that Auschwitz was our destination. Many, however, stipulated that we might go to a camp deep inside Germany because the new Nazi policy toward Polish political prisoners was not to eliminate them quickly but to first exploit their physical labor potential. This change of Hitler's policy became known to many of us. So it turned out that both opinions were correct. We were going to Auschwitz but for a short time to eliminate those unfit for work. From Kraków to Oświęcim (the name of the town, next to which this infamous camp was established) was around forty miles, yet it took another twelve hours or so for our train to get there. Somewhere at the midpoint of the distance, we crossed the border between the General Government and Deutsches Reich— in other words, between the territory temporarily left for Poles and that which was already annexed into Germany. The SS men became more relaxed while we, the prisoners, became more depressed. Here the intervention of the underground army was unlikely.

During this most uncomfortable, hungry, and humiliating journey, one could learn how inventive human beings could be in case of desperate need or desire. When we left the prison, by rule, we shouldn't have anything but our clothes, which were disinfected in a steam bath. However, some money and pictures were returned to us from the prison vault. Yet in our boxcar, certain people had pills, tobacco, and even a knife. What they did not have was food or matches. Of course, the SS guards were smoking. This tremendously stimulated the desire of the prisoners addicted to smoking. Some even started to beg for "just one smoke please!" The answer was always, "Shut up! Silence! *Verboten!*" The fellow who had tobacco got from someone a piece of paper and rolled a cigarette. He showed it to the SS man and asked for a match: "Fire, fire." He was lucky not to receive a blow from a rifle butt. He got only the answer "*Verboten!*"

Then a prisoner who looked like a peasant but seemed very smart said in broken German, "If you'll give me a cigarette, I shall light it!"

"How? Do you have matches? A lighter?"

"No, but I can make a fire."

That raised quite a curiosity.

One of the Germans said, "Good, if you'll make the fire, I'll give you a cigarette."

So the smart guy started to collect the necessary accessories: an old-fashioned metal button from a pair of pants, a three-foot-long string (or rather, a heavy thread), a small handful of cotton wool from the lining in his jacket, and his shoe with a steel heel protector. He placed the shoe upside down on the shoulder of the guy in front of him, who held it firm, and placed the wool about two inches from the heel protector. Then he threaded the string through the holes in the button and tied the ends of the string together. Holding each end of this double string on the thumbs of each hand, he started to spin the button, which was in the center of the string. By relaxing then stretching the string, the spin of the button increased. After he repeated this several times, the button was rotating with tremendous speed. Now he touched the heel protector with the spinning button. The stream of sparks burst out and hit the wool, which ignited immediately and kept glowing. Everybody was amazed with this performance, including both guards, who fulfilled their promise and gave a cigarette to our "Prometheus." He and a few of his neighbors enjoyed a few puffs of smoke.

It was getting dark when we got to Auschwitz. Through the open door of our boxcar, we could see in the distance a seemingly endless fence lit with electric bulbs on every post and interrupted every three hundred feet by watchtowers. A whispered commotion went through our car: "Brzezinka, Birkenau, not the actual Auschwitz."

"How do you know?"

"The original camp is in the old military barracks and is not so big."

"Is this better for us?"

"Who knows?"

"Are they going to give us something to eat? I hope we'll be in our beds soon!"

"This is such a big camp. How will they take us from the train to the barracks?"

The train was going back and forth, switching tracks. Finally, it pulled through a gate and stopped. After some whistles and shouting, our guards pushed the door wide open and jumped out. In no time at all, different SS men appeared in the door, shouting, "*Raus, raus, aussteigen, schnell!*" These shouts, repeated hundreds of times along the length of the train, filled the air. Bewildered prisoners jumped down from the cars onto the muddy ground. Those who hesitated or stumbled were hit or kicked by SS men standing on both sides of each door. A few steps away from the train, other SS men were rushing us to the lineup in blocks five men deep. And it was drizzling. The darkness was dimly lit by a few electric bulbs dangling in the wind above. And there was this terrible mud in which our legs were stuck.

The shouting, beating, and dogs barking and biting made this "welcome" in Birkenau absolutely terrifying. It took maybe fifteen or twenty minutes to form our blocks. At the end of each block, a few prisoners lay in the mud, disabled by violence, with broken or bruised legs from jumping from the car or caused by the blows of the guards. They had to be there, sick or dead, for the count of the *Häftlinge* must be complete and in agreement with the transfer documents. Counting was repeated several times because a prisoner from one of the cars was apparently missing. But they found him dead in the corner of a car. Finally, the documents were signed and exchanged, and new commands filled the air. "*Rechts um!*"—nobody understood it, so the shouting increased. And those standing in the first row were hit in the face and forcibly turned to face right. Here and there, we could hear this command shouted in Polish: "*W prawo zwrot!*" Finally, all 1,700 men turned as required, and the SS men shouted, "*Marsch! Los! Marschieren!*" And so began the most horrible walk of my life. Hungry, exhausted after a thirty-six-hour trip in devastating conditions, wet, wading in the mud, being guarded by the SS men and their dogs—it was an endless mile. How we all made it is impossible to answer. I was certainly in better condition to endure since I was well fed in prison, but 90 percent of the others had been hungry for months. I was also lucky to be in the center row, further away from the cruel escorts flanking our column. Whoever fell did not get up. He would be trampled by the block of men that followed, and if he survived this, when the last block of marchers passed, he was shot by the rear guard of the SS. Later, a special *Kommando* of already registered and uniformed Auschwitz prisoners collected the bodies.

We were going and going and going along the barbed wire fence when finally, we arrived in a large yard next to a large building. A barbed wire fence with one gate—behind which our SS escort remained—enclosed this compound. Most of us dropped to the ground, disregarding its condition, to take a rest.

For about one hour, nobody bothered us. Then a few prisoners who apparently were in charge of this "receiving facility" appeared. Those with more authority were in civilian clothing with red stripes painted along the seams of their pants and on the backs of the jackets. Their identification insignia was on the left chest of their jackets. This was a prisoner number (black on white) above a triangle of appropriate color (identifying the crime of the bearer) with a black letter (identifying nationality) on it. All this, of course, we learned later, including some exceptions (Germans did not have a letter on their triangle, and Jews wore a yellow star of David instead of a triangle).

Less important attendants of the receiving facility wore regular prison uniforms of German concentration camps (alternating light-gray and blue stripes running vertically). Their numbers and triangles were the same as described above. In the semidarkness, we did not see their faces well nor the letters and numbers on their chests. We could, however, hear well their shouts, swearing, and commands: "*Antreten! Antreten! Zu fuenf! Schnell! Schnell!*" When we were lined up in five long rows, one of them said something in German, then another one followed up with a speech in Polish. They wanted us to know that we had arrived at a fine camp where we could survive only if we followed the rules rigidly, obeyed the orders blindly, kept clean, and worked, worked, worked. He also told us that now we would get some food even though we did not deserve it. Then we would be registered.

Soon thereafter, they brought several kettles of "soup" and a few blankets loaded with small slices of bread. This food resembled very much the standard rations of our prison. They also brought one hundred to two hundred tin bowls—by far less than the number of our *Zugang*. This time, the command was "*Links-um*," and the five on the extreme left end of our column were to start the queue to receive a bowl followed by the soup and then a slice of bread. Soon tremendous chaos ensued. People were so hungry that many of them started to eat immediately after they got their rations, blocking the way of those who were behind them.

The pushing and swearing led to hitting and kicking, and in a short time, the hungry crowd was trying to drink their soup, chew their bread, and hold their ground while being pushed from all sides by others. In this turmoil, many lost most of their soup. Some lost their balance, fell into the mud, and were trampled under the feet of others.

The attendants soon interfered; with sticks, whips, and kicks, they moved the eating crowd further away, ordering them at the same time to eat their soup in a hurry because the bowls were needed for the others waiting in line. Some of the newcomers were ordered to collect the bowls and bring them for distribution at the head of the line. Those who had eaten their food were to assemble at the other half of the square and were watched carefully so they could not sneak back into the half where the hungry ones waited for their rations. Somehow, in this mess after our "dinner," I found my comrades from Cięszkowice: Jurek Kuhn and Władek Ptak. We had not seen one another in prison or during the trip to Auschwitz. From then on, we stuck together until Buchenwald.

Soon we were ordered to form a column again, standing in five rows one after the other. Starting to the right, we entered the door at the end of the building. Inside a long hall was a continuous row of narrow tables, behind which uniformed prisoners were standing with injection needles in their hands, at least a dozen of them. Next to the entrance door, at the beginning of the table, a few prisoners sat with armbands that said *Lagerstatistik*. Long lists of names in alphabetical order lay in front of them.

On their table were also a rubber stamp and an ink pad. Two SS officers were supervising this registration procedure. When I approached the table, one of the evidence men asked for my name, found it on the list, and stamped a consecutive number on the list and on my hand. Then I had to go to one of the guys with a needle. He tattooed this number under the upper part of my left arm. He was a Jew speaking conventional Polish. When doing his job of tattooing, his face was very close to my ear, so he told me in a low voice that it was unusual to put this number in such a hidden spot. Ours was the second thousand to get it there. This might be a good sign for us. And he was right; it had to do with the new Nazi policy of using prisoners for work in the same facilities where civilian people were working. The usual location of an Auschwitz prisoner number being on top of the forearm was visible, and so SS authorities decided to hide it. They changed their decision soon after because the new location was impractical. At each control point and whenever the identification of the prisoner was demanded, rolling up his sleeve and lifting his arm in an awkward manner to allow the reading of the number took time and irritated SS personnel. As a result, only three thousand Auschwitz prisoners got their numbers tattooed under the upper left arm. These were 152000, 153000, and 154000. These numbers were used for prisoners of two Zugangs (transports), one from Tarnów and the one from Warsaw, that arrived at Birkenau after ours in the early days of October 1943.

On the subject of these numbers, it shall be noted that they were tattooed on prisoners' arms only in Auschwitz. Also, it is important to know that the consecutive number does not reflect accurately the time of arrival of its bearer at the camp because many thousands of these numbers were reused after the original bearers' deaths. The highest number tattooed (I have not seen any number higher than 202,500) does not represent the total number of prisoners in all three camps under the Auschwitz command and administration because 95 percent of Jews, Gypsies, and Russian POWs were not numbered at all. Those were the people condemned to die within a very short time after arrival. There were exceptions, of course. I guess that the remaining 5 percent of Jews, Gypsies, and Russians were selected as extremely healthy and fit for hard work or because of some exceptional qualifications (doctors, artists, musicians, counterfeiters, and torturers). These people were given regular Häftlinge (prisoners) numbers and later used as it pleased SS authorities.

I was given number 153132, and it became my first and last name until I got another number in Buchenwald. Jurek Kuhn got a lower number, and Władek Ptak a higher one because the first one was ahead of me while the other was behind me. Once numbered, we followed the others and found ourselves in a big, strange-looking space. It resembled an amphitheater with tiers of seats circling some kinds of containers like tubs or sinks. The seats were single wood boards all supported on a wood trestle. Somehow we learned it was a sauna. In fact, it was still hot and humid when we entered it. But after it had filled to several times beyond its theoretical capacity with a crowd of dirty, stinky people, the atmosphere of this space became unbearable.

We were sitting on bench boards somewhere halfway up, tightly against each other, wondering when the entire structure would collapse and we would drop down on those fellows who were squeezed somehow between the posts and braces that were holding us up. Our predicament was intensified by terrible thirst. The soup, which was actually salty water, and the hot, humid air combined to cause an irresistible desire to drink. Ironically, or perhaps on purpose, there was no water in the bath. There were plenty of pipes, valves, and faucets but no water. Moreover, at each faucet, there was a sign in German and in Polish: "Not for Drinking—Poison."

Somewhere at the end of a corridor, there was a toilet where water was running, but the same sign was also there. Despite that, people were fighting to get some of this poisonous water. Because of the overcrowding in the sauna and in the corridor as well, I did not attempt to go there and remained thirsty.

We were all suffering in a semiconscious condition. Perhaps I was dozing or just daydreaming about a crystal clear brook winding within a fragrant meadow when suddenly there was the rumble of opened doors and thunderous shouts of "*Raus! Raus!* Get out!" which jerked us out of our lethargy.

Here it shall be informative to review the chronology of these events since our arrival at the Birkenau camp: My guess was that we arrived there at about 6:00 p.m. Unloading and procedures on the ramp took half an hour to one hour. The march along the east and north side of camp BII took about one hour, and the so-called rest, the distribution of food, and the receiving of numbers took three to four hours. Therefore, we found ourselves in the sauna bath sometime between midnight and 1:00 a.m. We were chased out of the sauna bathhouse, I think, around 5:00 a.m.

Hungry, thirsty, half asleep, and soaked with sweat, we ran out of the building. The fresh outside air hit us like a gulp of 190-proof alcohol. Its freshness was good, but the temperature terrible. The puddles of water in the mud were covered with thin ice. Several *Kapos* and *Vorarbeiter* (leaders of a working detachment or work group) rushed us along the building wall and ordered us to fall into the typical five-men-deep formation. The building was five hundred feet long.

"Attention! At ease! Attention! At ease! Three steps forward! Three steps backward! *Rechts um!* Turn around again!"—those were the commands that we had to learn this morning to understand and perform. This exercise lasted fifteen or twenty minutes. It certainly helped to knead the mud under our feet. It was now ankle deep. But suddenly, after the command "At ease!" all the Kapos and their helpers left the square, leaving us standing in our formation along the wall of the building. Minutes went by, and in no time, everybody was shivering with cold.

The unprecedented early frost was biting. We were afraid to break our formation; therefore, our movements were limited. Jumping in place or hitting the sides of our bodies with our hands did not help much. The terrible cold penetrated through our wet clothing then through our bodies to the bones and to the soul. The darkness became gray, the sky in the east brightened up, and we noticed some activity beyond the fence. The second hour was going by when the sun showed up above the horizon.

Its sight was encouraging, but it took another hour before we could feel its warmth. Our Zugang was still standing at ease. However, half of its members sank into the mud. Between eight and nine o'clock, a few SS officers showed up. They passed our column quickly and burst into the building. We heard shouting and the sounds of blows, and soon a few Kapos, foremen, and regular uniformed prisoners ran out.

The Kapos, in a fury and with horrible swearing, approached our column and ordered us to line up in the correct original formation. Those who could not get up, who were slow, and who were not in line were hit with fist, stick, or boot. All those hits, kicks, and blows could not move several of our comrades. They remained immobile in the mud. So the attending prisoners pulled them out and carried them to the end of the column. We had to close the file then stand at attention, and the counting began again.

In the meantime, another group of attending prisoners brought kettles with coffee and bread. This was our first formal breakfast in the camp. The slices of bread were twice the size of those in Tarnów and were more bread-like. The "coffee," however, was similar—burned grain and acorns. But it was hot. This breakfast and the rising sun soothed our discomfort. By 10:00 a.m., we were left unattended in the space between the building and the barbed wire fence. This fence was typical for all concentration camp fences: ten- to twelve-foot-high concrete posts with the upper end turned inward, spaced, say, three meters (ten feet) on-center, carrying ten to twelve strings of barbed wire and equally spaced. As a general rule, those wires were electrified. But here, however, there were no sentry observation towers along the fence. That indicated that it was an interior fence that was separating one part of the camp from another one. The building was of wood and very big. It housed the registration hall, the sauna facility, the laundry, the barbers, the shower hall, and the clothing storage.

There was not much dry area in this yard, where we were waiting for our unknown future. Fortunately, the sun was warm, and it helped dry our clothes. No one wanted to talk; we were too tired and hopeless. I remember only that someone was wondering how it was possible that so few of us collapsed during the past night. This was against all medical wisdom. All of us should have gotten pneumonia or at least severe coughs. Between 11:00 a.m. and 1:00 p.m., we had a very unusual show. On the other side of the fence, at a distance of about two hundred feet, we could see a few barracks. From those barracks, several woman prisoners brought out three or four tables and a few chairs, placing them more or less in the center of the area between the fence and those barracks. Soon thereafter, we heard shouts typical of SS officers escorting a walking column of prisoners. This time, however, these were women's voices. SS women were directing about two hundred women prisoners. They moved into the space beyond our fence, where the tables had been set. What a sight! The escorts were in typical SS uniforms except that they wore skirts instead of pants, and instead of helmets, they had field caps on their heads. Each of them had a whip in her hand and a pistol on her belt. Their faces were full of vicious excitement while shouting obscenities and looking to use their whips whereas their victims, the women prisoners, bewildered and completely naked, were running in small steps, packed closely together like a herd of sheep. They stopped about fifteen steps away from the tables. Then two SS women officers and a bunch of women Kapos approached them from the barracks. One of the escorts reported something to the officers, and all the escorts walked back to where they came.

The women prisoners, naked and yet somehow relaxed, started to mill around, awaiting further orders. The Kapo women were telling them something when a few SS men appeared. They, together with the women officers, took their seats at the tables, and one of the Kapos started to read names from the list. When she called a name, one of the prisoners approached the tables. Apparently, the female officer asked her a few questions while the SS men observed her from all sides. Then one of them pointed at something to the right and then to the left. What was the purpose of this selection? I don't know. Who were these women? I don't know. One thing was sure: they must have been captured recently because their physical condition was rather normal—not skeletons covered by skin, as was common for 90 percent of prisoners within a week after incarceration.

Another fact to be noted here is that we, the male spectators of this pitiful show, were so humiliated by it that we were watching it without any emotion. The only comment one could hear was that the majority of the women without clothing looked rather unattractive. The selection of female prisoners was still going on when I found a relatively dry spot on the ground and fell asleep. Three hours of rest considerably restored my physical condition. Then at about 4:00 p.m., we got our second meal: the soup—one liter of warm, salty water with some leaves floating in it. Immediately thereafter the Kapos of the *Badeanstalt* (bath facility) lined us up for the next procedures. Now we were to enter a room where we had to strip off all our clothing. Everything from head to toe as well as money, pictures, and anything we brought with us had to be formally deposited in the camp storage vault. The only item that we could retain was a leather belt. Everything was carefully recorded and packed. Since my clothes were terribly dirty, I was told that they would be washed before storage.

With belts in our hands, we proceeded to another room: the "barbershop." Here a number of prisoners worked as barbers. Some operated hand hair cutters, and others razors. Both of these instruments were equally dull. One barber would cut the hair on our heads off, leaving only a mane three centimeters wide and one centimeter high in the center that ran from the forehead to the back of the neck. The second one removed the hair from the armpits and crotch. This was particularly painful since the skin there is soft, the cutter was pulling rather than cutting, and the barber, a Russian, was being careless. A third one shaved my beard, and I had to make it soft by applying so-called soap. But in any case, it was not so bad because my hair was young and soft by nature.

Now hairless, we were assembled in groups of thirty or forty in the vestibule to the shower facility. Here each of us received a piece of clay called soap. It seemed to contain some kind of chemical because, to a certain degree, it helped remove the dirt. However, the washing procedure itself was a farce. It was a game of who succeeded in taking advantage of the unpredictable water supply within the available five minutes. Yes, time was the number one problem. With, say, forty showerheads to wash 1,500 people for five minutes each, it would take more than three hours, but that's in theory only. In reality, not all the showers were working, the people did not move like on a conveyor belt, and in particular, the water supply was irregular. Who knows why? Was the water supply system not functioning well? Or did the attending crew do it on purpose? Anyway, at times, there was no water at all, and other times, it was very cold or very hot. I got lucky. When I ran under my showerhead, the water was lukewarm, and I was able to apply the soap to most of my body. And then I got a sudden surge of unbearably hot water. I couldn't stay under it, but by splashing this water over my body with my hands, I could wash off most of the soap and dirt. Attendants with twigs did not let you stay in the shower for even a second longer. However, you had to remain in the same room where the showers were for a much longer time. It was hot and humid there.

We were supposed to dry off, but I was still wet when I was directed to run through a door to the next room. Here we got our camp clothes. I ran along a row of tables, behind which stood prisoners attending this facility. Behind them were piles of various parts of a wardrobe. When I approached the first of the attendants, he took a pair of boxer shorts from a pile and threw them on the table in front of me, which I had to grab, and then I ran further. At the next position, I got in an identical manner a shirt, and at the next one, a pair of trousers then a jacket then a pair of shoes. Nobody was paying any attention to my size. I had to grab in a hurry what was given to me and ran out of the room through a door opposite from the entrance, going out into the mud and the cold of the night. I ran further into the yard—in fact, as close as possible to the fence because there was more room not yet occupied by other prisoners and more illumination from the light bulbs on the fence.

The only piece of clothing that fit me were the trousers. The shorts and shirt were too large, and the jacket and shoes too small. How was I to put these things on? You could not free your hands of your belongings because the only place you could deposit them was in the mud surrounding you everywhere. Fortunately, Władek Ptak followed me, so we helped each other. He held his clothes and mine while I pulled on that oversized shirt. Then I held his and my belongings while he put on his shirt. We did this first because the cold was penetrating our bodies again. Naked and having gone directly from the heat of the bath into the freezing and windy outdoors, we were shivering so much it was difficult to put a hand into a sleeve. To pull the trousers on without losing my balance, I had to hold on to Władek, then he held on to me. Then we made some attempt to barter the ill-fitting items. For my shoes, I got wooden clogs. They were too big, but at least I could protect my feet from direct contact with the freezing mud and water. The chill of the night was getting more and more penetrating, so we got the idea to cluster together. Two or three such clusters of several hundred people formed, packed solid against one another. Certainly, it was much warmer within the cluster, but those on the perimeter were freezing and tried desperately to squeeze inward. Sometimes they exerted such pressure that the entire cluster was heaving and moving from side to side. This was dangerous. Some had their legs broken, and that was the end for them.

Before this macabre night ended, several Kapos appeared and forced us again, with shouts and sticks, into that five-man-deep column along the wall of the bath facility. When the sun rose, we were counted, including the dead corpses and the sick at the end of the column. Then the coffee and bread arrived. After this breakfast, we were called to order again. This time a few SS officers were present. An inspection of our appearance took place. I was ordered to put my jacket on. It was not possible because it was, perhaps, from a boy of maybe eight years old. They let me step out of the formation. There were a few others with similar problems. When all were called out, the Kapo of the *Waescherei* (laundry) ordered us to follow him. In the same clothing distribution area where we got our clothes during the night, he let us pick out such pieces that were of appropriate size. So I took advantage of the situation and also changed my shirt and pants. In this manner, I became fairly well clothed except for the shoes. These remained for a very long time a terrible nuisance for me. It could have been fatal, but more about that later. Soon after we were back in our ranks, a detachment of SS men arrived. We were counted again and ordered to march out of the registration and bath facility.

It was 10:00 or 11:00 a.m., approximately forty-two hours after our arrival in Birkenau. The day was cloudy and gray. However, we could see well the enormous expanse of the camp. We were moving along its northern fence in an easterly direction. On our right were rows of wooden barracks and fences perpendicular to our road, extending away for quite a distance. Between each two rows of barracks was a road with the entrance gate and elevated guardhouse at the road we were walking on. Some of those subcamps looked empty while in others, crowds of people were moving around.

To keep pace with the others and avoid a blow or a kick from the escort, I walked barefoot, carrying the clogs in my hands. But I had to put them on when our column stopped and the SS men demanded we line up in fives and instructed that from now on, we should march at an even pace while holding our hands along the seams of the trousers. Soon after the order to move on was given, the front of our column turned right to enter the gate to the last subcamp. When entering this gate, we were thoroughly counted by several SS officers: a *Lagerältester* (camp senior) and two *Schreiber* (clerks). The clerks and camp senior were prisoners assigned to perform these duties. We learned later that practically the entire internal administration of every German concentration camp was handled by its prisoners. The SS leadership decided about everything and supervised everything; however, inside the camp and on the work sites, prisoners nominated by SS authorities were responsible for the general order and the performance of all prisoners placed under their authority. Their authority was absolute and, as a general rule, ruthless. A common prisoner was totally at the mercy of his superior. Recourse was useless. After all, the primary intention of the Nazis was to destroy unwanted people and not to keep them in detention. Therefore, those who mistreated or killed a prisoner did exactly what was intended to be done.

There are official records and books describing in detail the degree of authority and responsibility of the many different camp enforcers. I shall mention them in the course of my story only wherever I became personally involved with some of these comrades with power. I may, however, express here my personal observation regarding who the SS leaders selected for certain functions were: the one in charge of the camp (Lagerältester), the one in charge of one barrack—where we slept (*Blockältester*), or the work group leader (Kapo), among others. In the great majority, those were prisoners of German nationality detained for criminal offenses. Next were German sex perverts then German political prisoners then Czechs, Poles, Jews, or others. It does not mean that all Germans detained in concentration camps were granted functions in the camp administration. They had to qualify for those as per SS standards and requirements. For some jobs, they selected utter brutes, and for others, professional experts. This German majority in the ranks of the camp's internal authorities was especially typical for Auschwitz, not so in Buchenwald.

One would think that they would have some confidence in those people. As per my observations, not necessarily! They forced them by terror to be obedient and efficient. Each such Kapo or Blockältester was responsible for his own skin for work or for the behavior of his subordinates. Punishments for the underperformance of all these camp enforcers were terribly cruel and often capital. There were also many prisoners of Polish nationality performing as Kapos but fewer as barracks seniors. The SS applied to them criteria similar to those applied to the German nationals plus the requirements of some knowledge of the German language. There was nobody among my friends in the concentration camp who would want to or were qualify to perform in any "leading," capacity and none were nominated to such position. Later, in Camp Dora, I was an exception to that rule; however, I shall write about it in chronological order. Many of the Polish prisoners, however, would dream about getting some function where survival was more likely—for example, being a Schreiber (i.e., a clerk in one of the camp's administrative offices) or a *Stubendienst* (barracks service man) or working in the kitchen, the clothing warehouse, or as physicians and sanitary personnel, who could work in the camp hospital, which was called the *Revier*. And in fact, many Poles succeeded in getting such jobs. But Kapos and Vorarbeiter (work foremen) were picked out from the criminal element present within the large mass of Polish prisoners, unfortunately, without distinction. Most of these criminals also got red triangles identifying them as "political." I have never seen a green triangle with the letter *P* on it, yet in each transport of inmates from any prison in Poland, there was probably 5 to 10 percent who were ordinary "lawbreakers."

In the subcamp where we just arrived, the "power" was in Jewish hands. The Lagerältester, all Blockältester, and even some Stubendienst were Jewish. Most of them were from the city of Łódz, which was renamed by the Nazis as Litzmannstadt and incorporated into the German Reich. Most likely they were within the first Jewish transports to arrive in Birkenau and were picked out very early to perform certain duties in the camp.

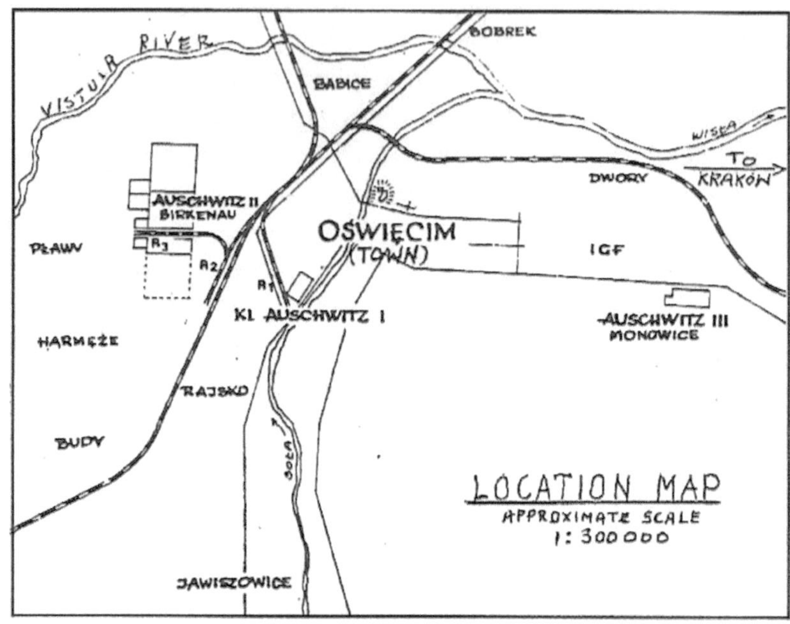

R-1   Railroad spur for KL Auschwitz I
R-2   Railroad spur for the unloading of Jews (Judenrampe)
R-3   Railroad spur within the camp Auschwitx II (Bikenau)
IGF   Construction site of chemical plant for IG-Farbenindustrie

LEGEND for the plan of AUSCHWITZ I

A   Residence of camp commandant
B   Main guard house
C   Camp Command offices
D   Camp Administration offices
E   Hospital for SS
F   GESTAPO offices
G   Camp Admitting facility
H   Arbeit Macht Frei – entry gate
I   Kitchen
KI Gas chamber and crematorium
L   Maintenance workshops & warehouses
M   Storage of goods robbed from prisoners
N   Gravel Pit – site of executions
O   Band stand
P   Laundry
R   Blockfuerer's offices
S   Death Wall
1 to 28 Blocks – prisoner's barracks

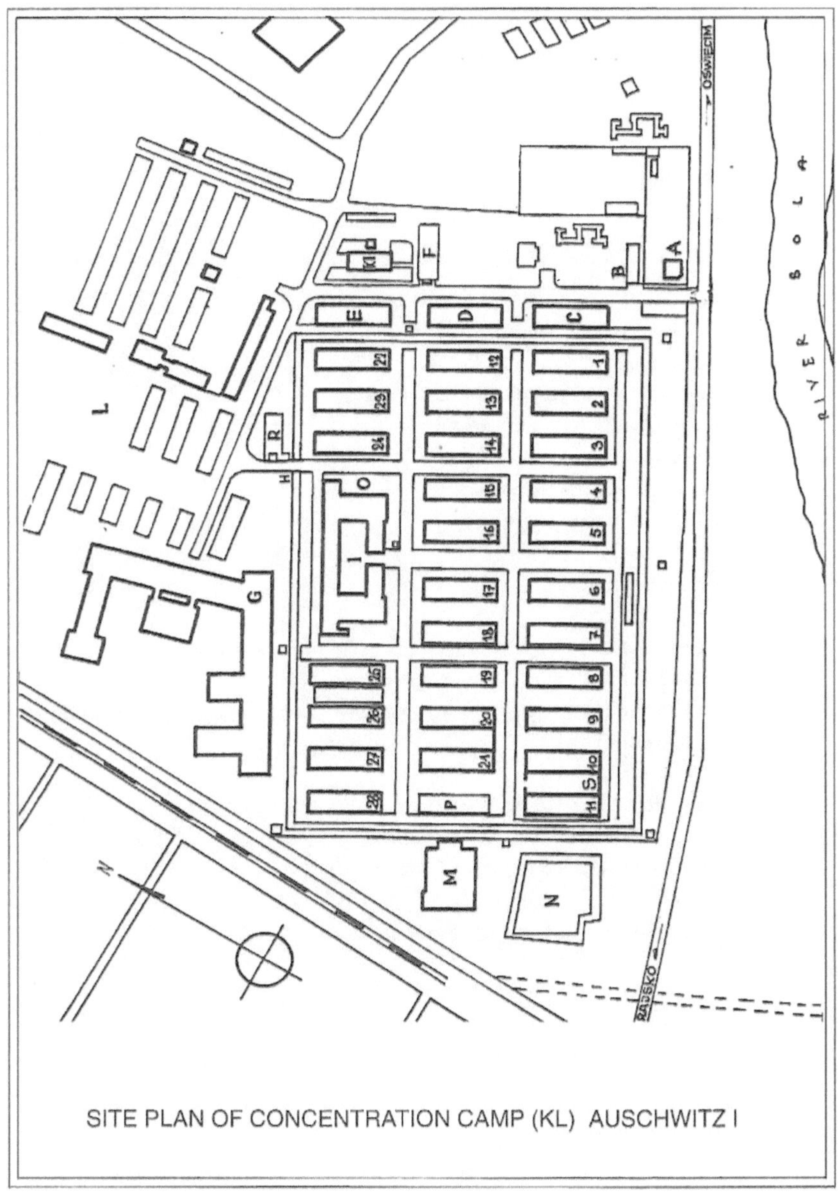

SITE PLAN OF CONCENTRATION CAMP (KL) AUSCHWITZ I

LEGEND for the plan of BIRKENAU

A	Main guard house with the tower
BI	Earliest part of the camp
BIa	for Women
BIb	for Men - later also for Women
BII	Second part of the camp
BIIa	Quarantine
BIIb	for Jews from Terezin
BIIc	for Jews from Hungary
BIId	for Men
BIIe	for Gypsies
BIIf	Hospital
BIII	Third part of the camp, under construction (Mexico)
C	Facilities for the SS troops
D	Warehouses for the goods robbed from prisoners (Canada)
E	Railroad platform
F	Bath facilities
G	Pits or piles where bodies were burned
H	Mass grave of Soviet prisoners
I	First (temporary) gas chamber
J	Second " " "
KII	Gas chamber and crematorium
KIII	" " " "
KIV	" " " "
KV	" " " "
L	Toilet facilities

SITE PLAN OF CONCENTRATION CAMP AUSCHWITZ II - BIRKENAU

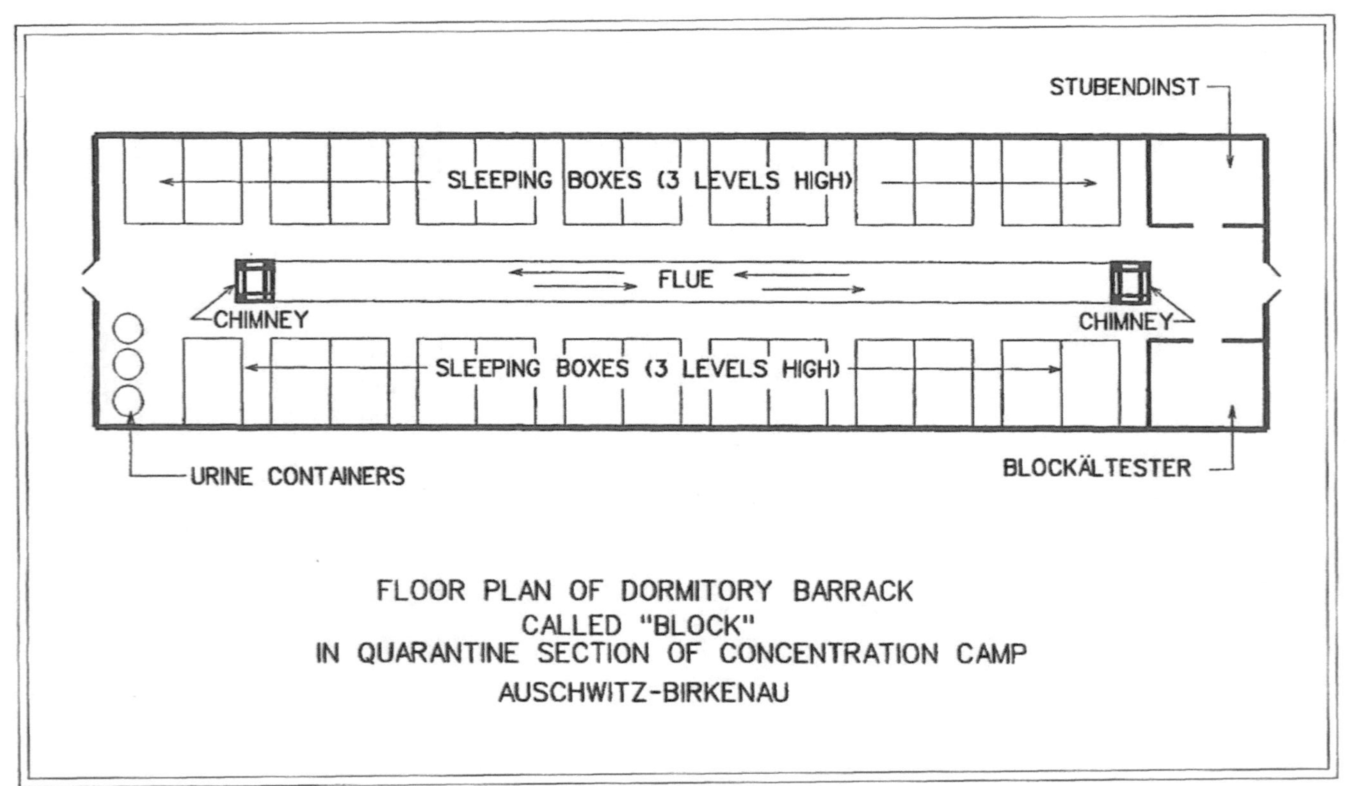

FLOOR PLAN OF DORMITORY BARRACK
CALLED "BLOCK"
IN QUARANTINE SECTION OF CONCENTRATION CAMP
AUSCHWITZ-BIRKENAU

CHAPTER 5

Birkenau Quarantine

Our subcamp, or division, of Birkenau was called quarantine. It was named this because it was supposed to be a place for the isolation of infected persons to prevent spread of diseases. However, the intention there was to teach us to be obedient and harmless Häftlinge (inmates), thrash us, and weed out all incapable of survival.

The quarantine division was a rectangle approximately 125 meters (400 feet wide) by 800 meters (2,600 feet long). The entrance was on the northern short side. A straight gravel road ran from the gate the entire length of the field. On the left there was an empty strip of land about 30 meters (100 feet) wide between the road and the exterior fence, along which six or seven sentry guard towers were located. On the right was one row of barracks with their gable (short) ends facing the road. There were eighteen of them, all erected at approximately the same distance from each other. Sixteen barracks housed prisoners whereas the two at the far end of the field were for common use—one as a washing facility and the second as a latrine. The living barracks was approximately 10 meters (33 feet) wide and 40 meters (130 feet) long. It was of wood framing and wood board siding. Wide doors were in the center of each short wall. Maybe 4 or 5 feet in from each door, there was a masonry chimney extending through the roof. An opening that looked like a fireplace faced the door. Both of these chimneys were interconnected with a double horizontal flue built of masonry. Its outside dimensions were about 3 feet high and 4 feet wide. This was a clever device to keep these buildings warm. Hot air and smoke from the fireplace at the front door had to travel the entire length of the duct to exhaust through the chimney at the rear door and vice versa. This design was for horses, for which such a barracks were originally intended. During the time I was there, nothing was burnt in this particular stove. It served an entirely different purpose. On both sides of this masonry duct were walkways about 3 feet wide, and between the walkways and the exterior wall, there were wooden sleeping racks. To my recollection, these racks were three levels high and about 6 feet deep and 7.5 feet wide. Fourteen of such racks on each side of the barracks provided eighty-four sleeping boxes. Now, since 720 Häftlinge were to sleep in one barracks, we had to squeeze eight or nine into each box, having less than a one-foot-wide space for each of us.

Jurek K., Władek P. and I, sticking together, got into block number 7. Our Blockältester, a husky Jew in his forties, was fluent in Polish and German. However, he used Polish very seldom. We nicknamed him King Herod.

It is difficult to remember what happened in this camp day by day. Sporadic visions float in my memory, which may illustrate the horror of the twenty days I spent there.

Twice daily, a roll call assembly, called *Appell*, took place—one before sunrise, the second before sunset. Upon whistles and terrible shouting, we had to run to the empty space between the two barracks and form a human block seventy-two men long and ten men deep. Since nobody wanted to be in the first row, exposed to all kind of abuses from SS men and Blockältester, there were fights for a more secure spot in the middle. Often, clubs by Stubendienst established order. No one could predict how long such an Appell would last. It could last one hour, two hours, or sometimes even longer. As usual, the formal purpose of the roll call was to determine if everybody was at "home."

They kept all ten thousand men in the quarantine camp standing until every single Häftling was accounted for. Of course, the sick and dead bodies had to participate in the roll call as well. The healthy comrades carried those to the end of the block. The real problem developed if someone died unnoticed in an inconspicuous spot. We would stand until his body was found. The Appelle were also used to teach us all kinds of lessons. For stealing food, sneaking into the barrack, sleeping during the daytime, losing a part of your clothing, or being dirty, people were flogged in front of all of us while standing at attention.

The most shocking show took place on the second day after our arrival. One of our fellows apparently could not stand it anymore and, in an attempt to commit suicide, ran and threw himself against the electrified barbed wire fence. He died there after being shot by the sentries from the tower. The SS men decided to use this incident to teach us that no one should attempt to escape from the camp. The body of this "fugitive" was put on display in front of our barracks, and during the next roll call, an SS officer came and gave a speech, which was translated by the Blockältester into Polish. The essence of this talk was that it was hopeless to attempt escape from any concentration camp under SS command. Who would try would be killed like this one. Moreover, for each fugitive, ten other prisoners from his block (barracks) or from his work Kommando (group) would be executed. Having said this, he proceeded to select ten victims from our still standing ranks. That was a horrifying experience: just standing there, totally helpless, and watching this cruel man walking in front of you and looking for who to pick out for death. It could be you, your best friend, or the guy standing next to you. The unfortunate guy who got picked had to step out of the file. Some of them became hysterical. The SS men would set the dogs on those. The beasts jumped upon the helpless victims, overturned them, and were about to bite their throats. But the SS men prevented this from happening and herded off ten of our comrades toward the road where they lined them along the ditch in a spot well visible to all of us. Then each of the SS officers pulled out his pistol and shot two prisoners in the back of their heads.

We were prohibited to walk. We were standing, or we were running. A walking prisoner was chased by Blockältester, Stubendienst, and, of course, by SS men, who, as a general rule, used their dogs for this purpose. A man bitten by a dog had little chance to cure his wounds in those circumstances. Getting in or out of the barracks was always connected with wild rushing, scary shouting, beating, and kicking. In particular, the morning rush to the roll call was very dangerous. People were suddenly woken up, half conscious, and moving blindly. Some moved in the right direction while others, confused, in the opposite. Others were getting out of their sleeping boxes, some jumping from the top one into the crowd below. Between those whirling streams of people on top of the masonry duct, our King Herod would run, furious, shouting obscenities and hitting right and left with a wooden stick or whip in his hand like a cavalry man during a charge. Many of these blows landed on my head, shoulders, or back. Fortunately, no bones were broken.

After the morning roll call, bread and coffee were distributed. Sometimes a little piece of margarine or a spoon of marmalade was added. The soup was distributed in the afternoon. That was the season for pumpkins. So with few exceptions, our soup was the water in which boiled pumpkin fibers were floating.

During our first day in the quarantine camp, we received our bowls, which were to be used for coffee and soup. The bowls in this camp were of a different shape and color. Each, however, could hold no more than one liter of liquid. It was important to keep such a bowl secure and clean. If you lost your bowl, you would not get your soup or coffee. If your bowl was soiled, you could be punished by the Blockältester in many different ways—by flogging, by reducing volume of the soup given to you, or by assigning you to carry out, empty, and clean the latrine buckets. Somehow, everybody managed to find a short piece of string or wire and attached the bowl to his belt to have it always with him. The cleaning was accomplished by using sand or any available dirt then rinsing it with water. Unfortunately, no matter how clean our bowls were, the quantity of food we received was insufficient. The hunger was getting more and more annoying the longer we were subjected to it.

That reminds me of an amusing but tragic event. The soup containers, looking like barrels with fifty liters of soup each, were brought from the kitchen by the not-hungry-looking kitchen Kommando. Two hundred containers were needed for our camp. To collect and to wash them and then to deliver back to the kitchen, a special Kommando was established. For some reason, the personnel of this work detachment was constantly changed.

One day, a group of Romanian Jews arrived to pick up our barrels. Apparently, the Nazis had mistreated these men already for a long time because there was no meat on their bones. In concentration camps, such walking skeletons were called *Muselman*. For some strange reason, all those Romanian *Muselmanen* had identical black suits, upon which the Star of David was shining bright. They were so terribly hungry that any crumb or drop of food was an irresistible temptation for them. So they would run like mad animals to grab an empty soup container and lick it clean. Accidentally, in one of the containers delivered to our barracks, the soup was heavier than usual. So after it had been taken outside, the inside of the container was covered with an unusually thick layer of pumpkin fibers. The fellow who grabbed this container noticed that treasure and took it from the crowd of his companions to a seemingly safe place between the barracks. Here, with his head, shoulders, and hands inside the barrel, he was scraping off and eating the remnants of the soup. His comrades, however, had noticed that he got something extra in that barrel, and several of them ran after him. Soon a scuffle started, in conclusion to which our lucky food hunter found himself inside of his barrel, which was pulled, overturned and rolled by his hungry friends. When he emerged out of the barrel completely covered by yellow-and-orange soup ingredients, he began running away, licking his sleeves. But a few Muselmanen abandoned the barrel and ran after him, scraping off the stuff from his body with their fingers and stuffing their mouths. Such a degradation of human dignity can only be understood by someone who himself was starving of hunger.

All three of us—Jurek, Władek, and I—stuck together and slept in the same box on the second level of the sixth rack on the right side from the entrance of barrack number 7. Of course, six other fellows shared that box with us. Meager remnants of straw were in each box as well as three dirty blankets. We could lie only on our side; for lying on the back, there was no room. Turning around to change the side on which one lay was almost impossible since we also shared one blanket. All three of us usually turned around simultaneously. Getting in or out of this den was a challenge also since it was accessible only from the front side. We prayed to God to keep us healthy, for any illness meant practically the end. In the best case, one could be taken to the camp hospital, but there were very few who got out of there. Even ordinary bowel movements presented a dangerous problem. There were latrine containers in the barracks near the rear door. Those, however, were for urine only. Relieving one's bowels was not possible because (a) it was prohibited, (b) there was no seat arrangement, and (c) men sleeping on the rack next to those containers would beat you up. Therefore, the only other option was the latrine barracks. It was a terrible place to use even during the daytime. Along both walls, there were wide benches with round openings cut out at two or three feet on-center, maybe fifty of them in one row. These seats were usually very dirty. Climbing up with your feet on these benches was prohibited. It was more convenient to sit on the single rail, which ran along both sides of the open trench in the center of this facility. It was cleaner but not safe. One could lose balance and fall back into this horrible trench. The smell of chlorine was overwhelming. But it was better than the stench of human waste.

Once I was forced to use the latrine during the night. This was no fun at all. Getting out of my sleeping box was a problem. Then I had to sneak out through the rear door because it was always dangerous to pass between the rooms of the Blockältester and the Stubendienst, which were by the front door. Then I had to go between the two barracks to the camp road and follow it to the end of the field. That was about 1,600 feet. Running along this road at night was dangerous because a sentry from a guard tower could shoot you just for the fun of shooting. I made it there all right and on time. Some, however, soiled themselves just getting out of the box, and many could not hold it while running down the road. Then, instead of the latrine, they had to go to the lavatory barracks to clean themselves and their clothes. This lavatory facility was another peculiarity. There were endless troughs with numerous faucets above them and with just a few showerheads, but the water was always cold and insufficient in quantity. Not to speak of how there was no time for washing. Even if in this building there were two hundred faucets, that meant about fifty Häflinge for one faucet. Between the rouse and the roll call, there were thirty to forty-five minutes, so if everyone washed themselves, he did not have even one minute to do so. But for those who really wanted to wash themselves, the real problem was lack of water. It was running only from a few faucets near the entrance. It was hopeless to get to those through a turbulent and angry crowd. For some purpose, there was a freestanding faucet outside the building. It was inaccessible in the early morning hours because a hill of ice would build up around it. Nevertheless, this was the place where I washed myself every morning.

They kept us busy most of the time. Cleaning the camp, the barrack, or our own wardrobe was often our occupation. Here I have to mention that there was a true effort by camp authorities to prevent the spread of some infectious diseases. The methods were inhumane, but disinfection was accomplished. Anyone who emptied his bowel not in the latrine was severely beaten. If someone found a louse on himself and reported it, his belongings were taken to a steam bath, and he himself had to wash thoroughly then was sprayed with some insecticide. However, he had to remain naked or covered only with blankets for twenty-four hours until his clothes were returned. When a louse was noticed on a prisoner by anyone with authority, in addition to the above procedure, he was punished by the Blockältester by forcing his head and shoulders into the fireplace opening then hitting him on the buttocks twenty times with a stick or whip. When three or more prisoners reported the lice, sometimes the entire barracks was subject to *Entlausung*. That meant that everybody had to strip off his clothing and leave it in the barracks, which then was tightly closed and filled for several hours with some kind of poisonous gas. During that procedure, the naked inhabitants of the barracks had to wash themselves and were sprayed. In other parts of the camp where "permanent" inhabitants of Auschwitz (not in transit) were interned, this procedure was simplified. All prisoners from an infected barrack had to go to the gas chamber, where they were poisoned together with their lice.

The most common occupation in the quarantine camp, however, was to "raise a mound." This was as follows: ten to twenty

Häftlinge were given shovels and ordered to dig a pit in the southern half of the camp field. All others were to carry the excavated dirt to the north end of the field and deposit it there, building a sizeable mound. The dirt was carried in our jackets, which, for this purpose, were put on reverse, so their backs were in front of our bodies. Holding the bottom of the jacket in our hands, we approached the pit. Here we got two shovels of dirt into the jacket, and holding it over our stomachs, we had to run about six hundred meters (two thousand feet), deposit the dirt on the mound, and run back to pick up another load. Soon it became one endless chain of silly-looking guys running in a circle with dirt one way and without it the opposite way. Most often I maneuvered so as to be the digger and not the runner. Here I was more exposed to the whips and sticks of the Stubendienst who ran the operation, but running in my clogs was absolute torture. But so was running barefoot on the gravel road. Not to speak of the SS dogs, which were often set on the Häftlinge who did not run smoothly and in line. When the pit became deeper, it was not as easy to throw shovels full of dirt up and into the jacket of one of your running comrades. If you missed, you got a hit. For the diggers, the situation was much better the next day when the dirt was carried from the mound to the pit.

A few times, I had the opportunity to be near the fence separating us from the adjoining subcamp to the west of the quarantine section. Surprisingly, it was apparently occupied by families. There were men, women, and children. All looked rather well—like normal human beings in their own clothing and not devastated by hunger. They did not want to talk to us, so we thought that these were people from Hungary or Romania, speaking entirely different language than Polish. Later I learned that they were Jews from Terezín in Czechoslovakia, and I wondered why they did not want to communicate.

Daily, a cartload or two of dead bodies was collected in our camp by the *Töten* Kommando (death detachment) and pushed a long way to where the crematoriums were located. I have not seen these installations called ovens. However, I felt their existence and activity. Most of the time, day or night, the sweetish smell of their smoke surrounded us. October weather was cold and wet, and the last time we saw the sun was on the first day in the reception bath facility. The air, saturated with fog or mist and mixed with the smoke from the crematoriums, was terribly depressing. Our physical condition deteriorated more and more, and our psychological endurance was weakening. Our thoughts and talk now almost exclusively revolved around food and the "ovens" (e.g., "Who will be the next to go there?")

Surprisingly, without any warning, after twenty days of "training" in quarantine, we were ordered to leave that camp. Nobody knew why or where we were going. The Blockältester chased us out of the barrack, and lined us up, this time in a formation only five men deep. The number of occupants from block number 7 shrunk by now to about six hundred. After counting and reading our numbers, we were ordered to turn right and march in formation onto the camp road. At least three other barracks did the same maneuver. Now our column, standing row after row, each person very close to one another, occupied the entire length of the quarantine camp road. Then the column started to move through the gate. Beyond the gate, SS soldiers joined us on both sides of the column—one pair of escorts approximately every twenty rows of prisoners as they passed the gate. We turned right twice and marched south along the fence of the camp field we had just left. Then we turned away from Birkenau and walked at least three kilometers, maybe more. The escorts were not too rough this time. Nevertheless, it was a torturous walk for me on account of my shoes. Despite the rags with which I wrapped my feet, walking was difficult and painful. Taking the clogs off was no good either, for the surface of the road was rough gravel. Finally, we approached a cluster of two-story buildings of common red brick. To our astonishment we were brought to the original Auschwitz Concentration Camp, which we entered through the famous gate with the lettering overhead that said, "*Arbeit Macht frei*" (Work will make you free).

The buildings there were of masonry construction and two stories high. On each floor, a corridor ran in the center with several large rooms on each side. In these rooms, there were many three-level-high wood beds. In each there was one chewed-up, straw-filled mattress and a rag for a blanket.

The three thousand prisoners, transferred from Auschwitz II (Birkenau) to Auschwitz I, were packed into three or four such buildings, two men to a bed and a few on the floor. Yet it was more comfortable than in the quarantine camp. Unfortunately, there was not much time to take advantage of the comfort. They kept us busy, distributing the soup (we still had our bowls, which we received in Birkenau), making us give up all our belongings (except the belt, as usual), giving us haircuts (the mane remaining), shaving us (our beards, armpits, and crotches), herding us to the showers (this time warm and effective), weighing us (my weight was ninety-two pounds—wow! I lost sixty-six pounds in three weeks), then having us collect our new wardrobe. This was organized well. Each item had its own stall, above which signs in German and Polish indicated size. At last, I got everything that fitted me fairly well. Only the jacket was what I needed to exchange. I was given a jacket with sleeves that were too short whereas somebody got one with sleeves too long for him. Now we had grey-blue striped uniforms that made us all look alike. We also received striped caps, called *Mütze* in German. And the socks, unbelievable! And the shoes! Hey! Hey! What a relief, no more of those damned clogs. However, those shoes were extremely primitive. The sole was still of wood, but the upper part was of canvas fabric, reaching up to the ankles and with holes for shoelaces. We were allowed to try on the first pair of shoes given to us to see if they were good on our feet and eventually exchange it for a better one if needed. I was happy with the first pair.

Nobody expected that this entire set of clothing, which we received in Auschwitz, would serve us for many months to come. This whole process of acquiring our "uniforms" went on and on from the early evening of the day of our arrival until noon the next day. We were in and out of our building two or three times. Early in the morning, coffee and bread rations were distributed. At this occasion, we received our new dish: a messtin with a cover that had a slot on the back for fastening it to the belt.

A few minutes after noon, the soup was provided. It was unusually early, and it was better than any that we had received until then. As soon as we washed our messtins, we were called to order. The local Blockältester were in charge, and each took under his command about three hundred men and proceeded with a semi military drill, teaching us all German commands and, most important, how we were to walk in formation at attention. That included keeping each row of five men walking in perfect alignment, walking all in step (i.e., everybody with the same leg forward, our step length half a meter shorter than normal) while holding our hands immobile along the seams of our pants and looking straight ahead or, if ordered, to the right or to the left. At least fifteen minutes were devoted to train execution of each special command. "*Mützen auf*" and "*Mützen ab*"—those orders meant "Caps on" and "Caps off," respectively. We were even arranged in our detachment according to our height. In the first file were the tallest ones, and in the last one, the shortest. Fortunately, Jurek, Władek, and I were almost identical in height, so we remained in the same row of five somewhere in the middle of the detachment. Then there was a speech from which we learned that we, the ordinary "Banditen," were transformed into the *anständig* Häftlinge (decent prisoners), and now we were the lucky ones going on a long trip to Germany, where we should work for the victory of Greater Germany. And then, oh, a surprise! Each of us got a half loaf of bread, some margarine, and a piece of sausage.

It was late afternoon when we heard brass band music and almost instantly with it the command "*Achtung! Rechtsum! Vorwärts marsch!*" Detachment after detachment began marching toward the gate, at which, on our right, there was a sizable group of SS officers and on our left, a big band playing very well some martial music. There were, for sure, more than one hundred prisoners in this band, all looking healthy, well clad, and blowing into shiny instruments. When the front of our detachment was about twenty-five steps from the gate, our commanding Blockältester shouted, "*Achtung! Mützen ab!*" We straightened ourselves up, took off our caps with our left hands, and marched like mannequins between the SS men and the band out through the gate with the inscription "*Arbeit Macht frei!*"

We had been in Auschwitz for exactly twenty-four hours.

CHAPTER 6

Buchenwald

The train trip from Auschwitz to Buchenwald took about fifty hours. However, although we were loaded in identical boxcars, it was not as oppressive as the one from Tarnów to Auschwitz. There were less Häflinge to a car, so we could move, change our position, and sit down in a more relaxed manner. There was also a hole in the floor in one corner of the car that served as a latrine. The door was locked, and SS guards sat on the roof of each car. Through the small openings near the top of the sidewalls, which served as windows, it was not possible to see much outside. Only the shouts of railroad personnel sometimes indicated the name of the station where we were stopped. Yes, more stopping than moving. During the night, we arrived at Wrocław, called Breslau by the Germans, and stopped there until morning.

During the early hours of this journey, the worst problem was the temptation to eat the food we received before leaving Auschwitz. Despite warnings that the trip would be long, most of the hungry prisoners could not resist this temptation and ate their portions soon after boarding the train. This was a terrible mistake! I know well how miserable their condition was at the end of our trip because despite having eaten my last piece of bread as late as twenty-four hours after our departure, at the end of the journey, I was hungry and very weak. With the passage of time, the lack of water was getting more and more trying. Before noon of the second day of the trip, we became impatient, and at each occasion when the train was stopped and we heard someone near our boxcar, we screamed, "Water! Water!" Finally (I think it was near the railroad station in Görlitz), they let us have some water. The door opened, and one SS man took four men from our car to bring the water in buckets. The second SS man remained on guard at the open door. Fortunately, the train was standing so long that a second round of buckets of water was allowed. I succeeded in retaining some of the water in my messtin.

Officially, we were never told where we were going. However, since it became clear that we were heading straight west, we started to speculate that our destination was Buchenwald. That caused general relief because camps in Neuengamme and Sachsenhausen (north) or in Mauthausen (south) were considered much worse than old Buchenwald. *Old* because it was established at least two years before the outbreak of World War II, destined in particular for certain insubordinate Austrians and Czechs.

One passenger in our boxcar had a particular concern: "How will I be treated in the camp where my brother is a member of the SS detachment supervising this camp?" What a tragedy, but it was not unusual for many Silesian families. His name was Forster. His father was German, and his mother Polish; they had three sons, all born in the same Silesian mining town. However, the oldest one was born before World War I, when the town was within the borders of Germany. The two younger ones were born when it was part of Poland. Not surprisingly, their allegiance was corresponding. The father and the oldest son were German while the mother and two younger boys were Polish. It was endurable during peacetime, but when the war between these two nations broke out, the family fell apart. The parents remained in Silesia, but one son joined the SS whereas the two other brothers went east with the Polish army. The youngest found himself in the General Government and joined the Polish underground movement. For this, he was now a prisoner. The third was captured by the Soviet Red Army as a Polish soldier. Did he survive there? I don't know. I do not know if Mr. Forster, the Häftling, ever met his brother, the SS man.

After our nighttime arrival at a big railroad depot, some of my comrades told me it was Leipzig, and some said it was Chemnitz. For me, it was not important as I was weary and indifferent. I squeezed myself along the wall and fell asleep. When I woke up, it was a bright day. To my surprise, the door of our car was open, and one SS guard was sitting on the threshold with his back to us and his legs dangling outside. Balmy outside air was refreshing our boxcar. The train was rolling through beautiful hilly country. The prevailing beech trees were in brown-reddish foliage, which served as a backdrop for every pine or fir tree to shine with its bright-green needles. "Anhalt, Thuringia," informed someone familiar with the geography. Such a picturesque, peaceful-looking land. It was hard to realize that it was surrounded by a terrible, merciless war and that we are not tourists but prisoners. The hunger and thirst were now unbearable, but it was almost time for us to disembark. And sure enough, our train finally rolled to a stop in Weimar! Weimar, the town where mastery of life became the chief concern of Johann Wolfgang von Goethe, the giant of world literature and pillar of civilization…what would he write if he knew that thousands of innocent people were being brought to his beloved town as dehumanized Häftlinge?

A company of fresh SS men was waiting for us on the arrival platform. We were arranged as usual in a "five in row" formation and ordered to march. It was a very slow and tiring march. It was ten or twelve kilometers of uphill road from Weimar to Buchenwald. It did not matter that the road was convenient, wide, and of hard smooth surface; it did not matter that we were treated almost like human beings, without unnecessary shouts, hits, and kicks and that they let us rest every two kilometers; and it did not matter that we got water to drink before leaving the railroad depot. After so many hours of confinement in a boxcar, we were stiff, weak, and hungry. Behind our marching column, a truck followed, which collected those who collapsed. Keeping in mind Auschwitz's habit of disposing those weaklings, we were afraid to falter and kept moving.

It was pitch-dark when we arrived at Buchenwald and had been left sitting or lying on the concrete of the Appellplatz. While we were resting, totally exhausted, local prisoners were busy dividing us into groups of two hundred or three hundred each, bringing in kettles full of hot soup and distributing it to all these groups. I was astounded by the swift organization as well as the quality of the soup. It was a substantial semiliquid of beans or peas. One liter of this liquid put life back into my body. Now each group was given the number of the block (barracks) that would be our quarters, and a local Blockältester took command over us. He led us first to the latrine and washing facility, where we could wash our dishes and our faces. Then we went to our block (I think it was number 115). It was again a wooden barracks; however, it was of a different construction than that in Birkenau. Basically, it was smaller; however, there was more room per person. We slept well that night.

On the next day, our roll call was later than the one for Buchenwald's permanent inmates. After counting us and verifying our Auschwitz numbers, we had to go to the Buchenwald registration office, where we received our new numbers: Władek Ptak got 34183, Jurek Kuhn 34184, and I 34185. Each of us got two of these numbers printed in black figures on stripes of white cloth. In the next sizeable room were so-called tailors. Their job was to sew one number on the jacket on the left chest, just above our red triangle, and the other one on the right trouser leg, about fifteen centimeters above the knee. Then we went to the shower and back to our barracks.

Here, our Blockältester, a Czech, told us that we were in this camp in transit only. For now, we should be confined to the few isolated barracks in a sort of quarantine. Until this quarantine was lifted, we would not be called to any work, and we should take advantage of these few days, resting and regaining strength for the labor that awaited us in many of Buchenwald's subcamps, where we would be sent within a week or so. He also informed us that we could take advantage of the allowed postal service and write letters to our families. Obviously, I took advantage of this and sent my foster parents the first direct message after my arrest. All letters from and to concentration camps were subject to censorship. They had to be written in German and in legible lettering. I had to ask a fellow prisoner who could write in German to do it for me. It was appropriate to pay for his service. But with what? I offered a slice of bread; however, it was seldom taken. The majority of educated, intelligent people, even in concentration camps, preserved enough Christian charity to help one another on credit: "You'll give me something when you get a parcel from home." And in most instances, such debts were paid.

Our Blockältester was a decent man who expected from us order and obedience but acted without violence—no club, no whip, not even shouting. So were most of the Czechs who, in those days, for practical reasons, virtually ran the camp Buchenwald from within. The Lagerältester, most of the Blockältester, and many Kapos were all Czechs. They favored the Russians and kept them working in the kitchen, warehouses, and all kind of camp shops. There was only one problem with those Czechs. They did not like Poles and considered us anti-communists (correctly) and backward conservatives (incorrectly). Nevertheless, many Poles were employed in Buchenwald's administration—in particular as clerks, medical personnel, and musicians. One of those musicians was from Kraków and knew the Khun family. He had been notified that Jurek was captured and sent to Auschwitz. Therefore, he quickly found our friend and reassured him that his stay in Buchenwald would be better for him. He then made all necessary arrangements in the office of the *Arbeitsstatistik* to remove Häftling number 34184 from the quarantine and employ him in one of the permanent work squads of Buchenwald. And so it happened that I lost my dear friend Jurek Kuhn forever. Because even though he had a better life for that one year than Władek and I, he got lost during the evacuation of Buchenwald. According to a story told to me after the war by an eye witness, his evacuation train was standing at a railroad station when it was bombed by an Allied air raid. However, it is not clear to me whether he was killed by a bomb explosion or shot by a guard while attempting to escape.

This one week of quarantine in Buchenwald was beneficial for us—better food, no work, and no demoralizing mistreatment. This, coupled with the unusual warm weather, replenished our strength. So on November 2, 1943, we were in fair physical condition and in good spirits when we got the order to go. Two hundred men from our barracks were loaded on military transport trucks and driven almost a hundred kilometers northwest to Dora-Mittelbau.

CHAPTER 7

Dora-Mittelbau

We were crowded tight under the canvas top of the carriage whereas the open rear end of the truck was occupied by SS guards. So we did not see the landscape outside; only the movement of the truck indicated that the terrain was rolling. In about two or three hours, we arrived at our destination. Instantly we felt as if we were back in Birkenau. A muddy flat area at the foot of a steep mountain, barely visible through mist and fog, was surrounded by two wooden barracks and a number of tents. Before our guards even stepped off the truck, others outside started to shout, "*Raus! Raus! Aussteigen! Antreten! Zu fuenf! Zu fuenf! Schnell! Los!*" They counted us quickly. "All two hundred here! No sick, no dead! *Gut! Links um! Marschieren!*" It was a short walk from the provisory roll call square to the mouth of a tunnel.

In the tunnels

The approach to the tunnel, at least two hundred steps long, was cut into the mountain slope. It was sliced with several sets of railroad tracks. We stumbled on the ties and struggled in the mud, but the column of two hundred Häftlinge, surrounded by SS men, was moving swiftly. The black arch of the tunnel entrance was awaiting us. At the entry, there was a little guardhouse and a barrier of wood rail or steel pipe painted white, red, and black. Our escort reported something to the sentry in the guard booth, who lifted the barrier.

"March!" And we entered the grave. The abrupt change from light to dark made it hard to see. The stumbling became more dangerous, yet the shouts of *"Los! Los! Bewegen! Schnell!"* became louder and somehow more frightening. But who was shouting? The SS escorts remained outside, behind the barrier! Then we noticed them: it was a Kapo assisted by four or five Vorarbeiter. They now took command over the new Zugang and were leading—or rather, chasing—us into a horrifying, dusty darkness.

After slowly getting accustomed to the darkness, we noticed electric lights gleaming high above our heads. We were now walking on the paved platform, running for an unknown distance along two railroad tracks to our left and an uneven but solid wall of rock to our right. I say *unknown* because the cavern was filled with dust. A white-grayish looking fog was getting denser the deeper we moved into the tunnel. Near the entrance, we could see six or seven light bulbs in a row, but when we were two hundred steps further in already, the third one was hardly visible. And there was a noise that was increasing together with the amount of dust.

At a point when the noise and dust became almost unbearable, the rock wall on our right suddenly ended, and an enormous manmade cave appeared. Here was the source of the dust and noise. A crowd of people were working there. They quarried the rock, making a new tunnel perpendicular to the one in which we were walking. Several diesel-driven air compressors were supplying compressed air to numerous pneumatic hammers used to drill deep holes in the rock, in which dynamite would be placed to blast the rock. Both compressors and hammers were making a terrible noise that, reflected by the stone surfaces on five sides, was multiplied many times over. Hammering out the holes produced some dust, and crushing rocks with sledgehammers also contributed to the dust. But the real surge of dust came with each blast of dynamite. Since there was no air movement in such a cave, the dust simply hung there. Everything was covered by it: compressors, wheelbarrows, and people! Oh yes, the people—those little gray figures, some operating pneumatic hammers and sledgehammers while others were pushing wheelbarrows. The majority were collecting rock splinters with their bare hands and dropping them into the wheelbarrows. And a few were running the show with sticks and whips. In the hellish noise of the machinery, one could not hear any shouts, orders, screams of pain, nor any groans of agony. That glimpse into hell was intensified at the next cross tunnel. This one was much more advanced in its construction, not only being twenty-five to thirty feet high but also as much deeper. It looked like the inside of an enormous pipe. A few cranes and other stone-loading equipment stood on the floor, lifting boulders and crushed rock onto a conveyor carrying it above our heads to the open boxcars standing on the rails to our left. However, the buckets of those cranes were filled manually by hundreds of little grey figures swarming like ants among the machinery. On the far end of this pipe, they just dynamited the rock, and a cloud of dust was enveloping the tunnel and everything in it. But everything continued in motion without letting up—ants, clouds of dust, noise, clubs, whips, and screams. It was truly a macabre sight, something not of this world. I was appalled and truly scared, imagining that soon I would be working in this quarry, in this hell.

The next cross tunnel was already cut through. Here, the prisoners were working on scaffolds, chiseling off loose pieces of rock from the walls and ceiling. Occasionally, a huge rock splinter would break off, crushing the scaffolds and workers. Of course, a destroyed scaffold was a problem, but the dead prisoners…never. We walked past two or three more cross tunnels and turned into the next one, which looked completed. Here, we were ordered by our Kapo to change our formation. He wanted it to be according to height. So the five tallest guys would be on the right end of the corridor, and the five shortest on the left end. In between, of course, the height of prisoners would vary gradually. Władek Ptak and I were of the same height, so we were always in the same row of five, situated a bit right of the center of the entire column. We were told that from now on, we must assume the same place during each roll call and that this would be the new work group called Beton Kommando 2 (apparently, there was a concrete detachment number 1). We would be concreting floors in the newly built tunnels. It was the duty of our Kapo, Hans, to keep us in order, make us work efficiently, and distribute among us our daily ration of soup. The work in the tunnels of Dora was twelve hours per day except only six hours on Sundays. We would be working under the supervision of professional German civilians whom we must obey blindly. If not, our Kapo would take care of us.

By 6:00 p.m., it was time for the soup, and Hans organized its distribution. After the soup break, we might have to start working. The soup was not as good as that in Buchenwald, but it was much better than the water we got in Tarnów or Birkenau. After the meal, we were shown where the water was. The one available faucet was quite a distance away. We realized immediately that washing would be a problem here. One would be lucky to have a cup of water for drinking. While we were attempting to clean our canteens, the Kapo was looking for work for us. He found something for about fifty men. The rest were washing, standing, or sitting on the concrete floor. By now we started to feel the particular chill of these tunnels. I think that there was a constant temperature of fifty-three to fifty-seven degrees Fahrenheit, which was cold even when the air was calm. But wherever there was a draft, the cold penetrated our miserable uniforms, cutting to the very bone. We were constantly shivering.

Before I continue my tale, let me explain this concentration camp called Dora. Dora was a cryptonym for the official name: KL Mittelbau I. This camp was located just south of the Harz Mountains, about five kilometers northwest from the city of Nordhausen. In 1936, long before it became a concentration camp, the German chemical industry, following the plans of the German government, started to build on this site an underground warehouse for gasoline, oil, and explosives. In 1943, German officials decided to convert this warehouse into the assembly plant for V-2 rockets. This required the extension of the existing facility. Inasmuch until then, the warehouse was built in secret using German labor, and it became clear that to speed up construction, it would be necessary to use foreign workers. This constituted a serious threat to the secrecy of the project. Therefore, a logical solution was to establish a concentration camp there, filled with the cheapest labor and isolated from the outside world.

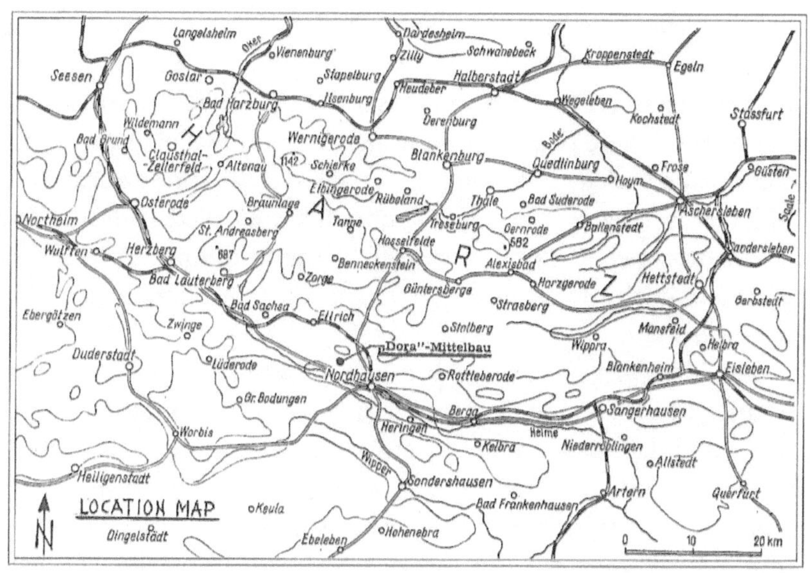

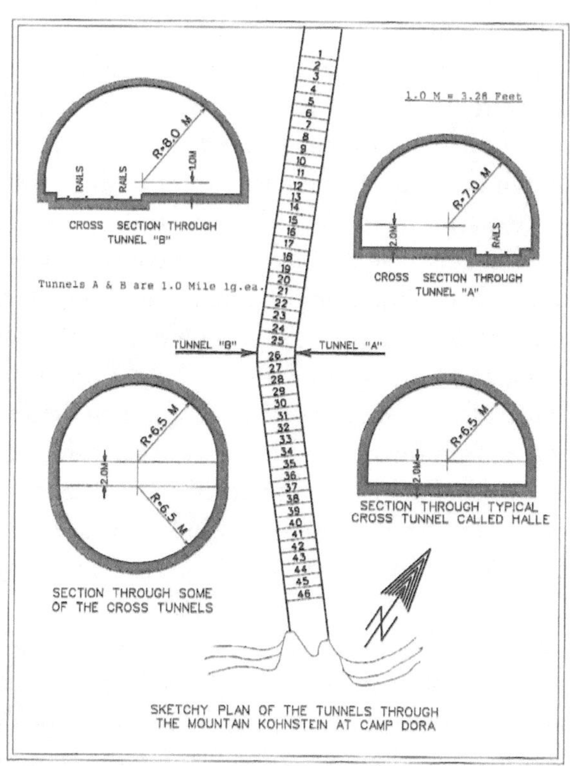

SKETCHY PLAN OF THE TUNNELS THROUGH
THE MOUNTAIN KOHNSTEIN AT CAMP DORA

It is difficult to visualize the enormity of this facility. It was all carved out of lime rock within the mountain called Kohnstein. I made a sketch that illustrates and describes this underground factory. Basically, there were two 1.5-mile-long tunnels parallel to each other, interconnected with forty-four or forty-six cross tunnels, each 325 to 425 feet in length. These cross tunnels were called *Halle*. Each of these tunnels was 40 to 50 feet wide at the floor and up to 30 feet high. There were a few ventilating shafts cut vertically up to the top of the mountain.

The first prisoners were brought to Dora from Buchenwald in August 1943. At this time, the tunnels were completed from the north and ended down to about cross tunnel number 30. Tunnel B was cut all the way to the south end, and tunnel A only down to Halle number 40. When I arrived in November, cross tunnels numbered 31 through 39 were cut out but not finished; in number 40, they removed loose rocks; number 41 (two stories high) was under construction; and in number 42, the cutting just began. Halle numbers 36, 37, 38, and 39 were used as sleeping "blocks" whereas numbers 31 through 35 were available for concreting and also for the roll calls. In the old portion of the tunnels, near the north end, partitions and rack systems, which were needed for warehousing, were removed. Within half a year after my arrival, the remainder of tunnel B and all Hallen were cut and completed. During the construction work in the south end, all the north-end Hallen were furnished with the machinery and equipment necessary for the production of V-2 rockets. After this assembly plant started to operate in the early summer of 1944, tunnel A was used for the delivery of parts and raw materials whereas tunnel B was the assembly line, which is as a platform moved on rails from north to south. The rockets were assembled by adding at each Halle various prefabricated components. However, V-2 rockets were shipped out of Dora in three twenty-foot-long parts, never totally assembled to their total length of sixty feet.

Of course, to have the entire tunnel system available for production, it was necessary to build barracks outside, near the entry to the tunnels. This work was in progress simultaneously with tunnel-cutting. Ultimately, there were more than one hundred barracks built, fifteen of which were occupied by the eighty-eight troops. Fifteen were used for administrative and housekeeping purposes, and the rest for housing prisoners. This camp was located just west from the south entry to the tunnels. Many of the blocks (barracks) were located already on the slope of the mountain, among the trees of preserved forest, and the entire plan of the camp was worked out with considerable attention to aesthetics. I believe that a German political prisoner was in charge of the camp construction and deserves the credit for this. The prisoners' camp was, as usual, surrounded with an electrified barbed wire fence and watchtowers equipped with powerful searchlights and machine guns. However, the second line of fencing surrounded a much larger area including the railroad depot, the SS barracks, and the entrance to the tunnels.

The internal "power" of this camp lay in the hands of criminal inmates, as in Auschwitz but unlike Buchenwald. The decisive majority of camp positions (Lagerältester, Blockältester, Kapos, *Lagerschutz*, etc.) were held by bandits, robbers, thieves, and perverts, all predominantly of German nationality. This, of course, resulted in the harshness of our life. Fortunately, there were functions that required other skills besides brute force, so all physicians, accountants, clerks and artists were political prisoners. And of course, skilled labor was required for the construction of buildings and roads within the rocket assembly plant. This group was called Savatzki Kommando. They were under the control of the engineer Albin Savatzki, who was the CEO of this plant. The struggle between brutality and performance was uniquely characteristic of the Dora concentration camp.

Forced by circumstances, the German headquarters began pressing for production with the realization that tired, hungry, and brutally beaten persons would not perform. Therefore, they demanded that working prisoners be treated more humanly. On the other hand, the SS did not want to give up on the Nazi philosophy, whereby all non-Germans should be considered as *Untermenschen*, who should be persecuted and destroyed at any occasion. So the life of a prisoner in a professional Kommando was much better than in those Kommandos handling ordinary work. When the work in factories was in high gear, it was, for the prisoner, better than when such work slowed down or ceased. As long as a Häftling was obediently working and efficient, no one touched him. However, if he became unproductive or committed some illegal act, he was mercilessly persecuted.

Now, back to my personal experiences. About thirty minutes after midnight, my first Appell in the tunnels began. This was the after-work roll call, one of two daily performed by each block (sleeping quarters) to determine how many Häftlinge would be (or were) accommodated there. We were assigned to the block B-3 in Halle number 37 and were to wait for all the other Kommandos dwelling in B-3 to arrive and join the formation. And arriving they were. Some of the guys were small and looked tired but fair while the others were big but completely worn out. The bigger guys came from the tunnel construction site, gray from dust, dragging their feet behind them, and some were carrying their sick and dead comrades. It took quite some time for them to line up because all living prisoners had to get in line, yet many simply could not stand. When neither a hand from a neighbor or blows by the Kapo or Blockältester helped, the sick man sank to the ground, where he was adjudged dead. He was then pulled by his legs to the end of the Kommando, where all immobile bodies were assembled.

Then they started counting. It took time because up to 1,200 Häftlinge could be in one block. It took time when a Kommando was late. But the real delay of procedures occurred when prisoners were missing. And that happened time and again. Exhausted men hid in some inaccessible corner and died there. Others were buried under the falling rocks while some drowned in a latrine. It took hours to find such a body, and the entire block had to wait. Every Häftling must be accounted for no matter healthy, sick, or dead. I do not remember how long that first Appell in the tunnels was, but an average after-work roll call lasted more than two hours whereas those before work seldom exceeded one hour.

When, finally, they let us go to our block, those guys who had already slept there and were familiar with the conditions in this "dormitory" started to rush; those who could run did so. We, the new Zugang, were slow because we did not know that on this block, one did not have his own bed. Whichever one you grabbed was yours for that night only. Even more important was to secure a blanket for yourself. There were always less blankets than beds. If you were late, you could sleep without a blanket somewhere at the end of the block whereas it was much better to be near the entrance, closer to food, closer to latrines, and closer to the Appell Halle.

One could appreciate better the size of the Halle when seeing it "furnished" with our beds—two aisles with racks four levels high on both sides in seemingly endless rows. The racks were built of wood with four beds on each level. Each bed was 2'6" wide and 6'2" long. All sixteen beds together constituted one rack that was 9'10" long, 6'6" deep, and 8'2" high. There were some spaces left between the racks. I never counted how many racks were along one aisle, maybe twenty on each side. To clarify the situation, I have to mention that these Hallen, used as accommodation blocks, were not open to tunnel B and were accessible only from tunnel A.

The crowding at the entry to the block became unbelievable. Because those who arrived first were squeezing themselves into the beds nearest to the entrance and as half of the beds were accessible from the aisle end only, they blocked the way for those who had to go deeper into the block. During these invasions of the dormitory, there was always a lot of shouting, swearing, and sometimes outright fighting among the prisoners. It took up to one hour for this turmoil to calm down.

Somehow I managed to stick together with Władek, and finally, we claimed our beds on the first level of a rack, which was maybe tenth from the entrance. The Stubendienst informed us that for each two levels of beds, one Häftling was to go pick up our food. He had to have with him the numbers of all eight guys to whom he would bring and distribute the rations. That became a big problem. How was he going to remember all these numbers? There was no pencil and no paper. If we had known ahead of time, something could've been organized. But this was the first time. Fortunately, we were all from the same transport and all our numbers began with 34, so the last three digits were somehow remembered by the fellow we elected to go for the rations. It could be disastrous for him if he gave a wrong number to the Schreiber and that name was already marked off; there would be one less portion to return with. As a suspect of cheating, he (the food carrier) could have been severely beaten.

After a long while, he came back with our precious, longed-for rations. In addition, there was distribution of bread, margarine, the four-times-per-week marmalade, the twice-a-week slice of sausage, and the once-a-week slice of cheese. The bread we received would be one loaf for eight prisoners. That was approximately 2.5" × 2" × 6" per person. A piece of margarine was 1" × 1" × 1/4", and the marmalade ration was one spoon.

Cutting of the bread and dividing it into absolutely identical eight pieces was the most solemn ceremony. It had to be done before the eyes of all individuals involved, who, with breathtaking attention, observed every move of the cutter and every crumb of bread. Sometimes I wondered, was Jesus Christ in a concentration camp before He instituted the sacrament of Holy Eucharist? He wasn't, but certainly He must have been once very hungry and understood very well how desirable a piece of bread is for a hungry man. Therefore, He wanted His word to likewise be desirable for us.

The bread-cutting and food-distribution ceremony was easier for the occupants of the upper level of a rack because all eight of them could assemble on the top level, where there was plenty of headroom and a sufficient amount of light. But those on the lower levels had to do it in confinement and darkness.

Russians turned out to be the most accurate in equal distribution of goods. Many of them managed to construct scales with which one could weigh one piece of bread against another. When all eight portions of bread were of identical weight, their mistrust still compelled them to draw lots. For this purpose, each had a number from 1 to 8. One would be blindfolded while someone else would point to a bread portion and asked him, "*Komu?*" (For whom?). Then the blindfolded one would call out, "Vtorayamu!" (For the second one!) or "*Pyatomu!*" (For the fifth one!) and so on until all eight received their bread. From then on, for several months, whenever bread was distributed, we heard those shouts—"*Komu?*" "*Pervomu!*" "*Vtorayamu!*" "*Tretiymu!*" etc.—for an hour or so.

To recap, it took two hours for the roll call, which started at 12:30 a.m., then came a one-hour fight for beds and blankets followed by the acquisition and distribution of the food—another hour. That would get us close to 5:00 a.m. Between 5:30 and 6:00 a.m., they distributed hot coffee, which we drank right away. Finally, around 6:00 a.m., we could lie down to sleep. Here I have to mention that whichever shift we worked—noon to midnight or midnight to noon—it always took at least six hours before we could get some sleep.

Yet at 10:00 a.m., there was wake-up rouse. At 10:30 a.m., there was roll call before work. At 11:30 A.M., we marched out to work. During the first few months in Dora, such sadistic disorganization of our resting time was, for me, the most devastating aspect of life. Three or four hours of sleep per day was not enough. It impacted my health and frame of mind more than hunger, poor sanitary conditions, cold, dust, or hard work.

Concreting was going on in several places throughout the tunnels. So our Kommando was split into several groups, each under the leadership of a Vorarbeiter. Władek and I were in a group working in tunnel A. A big concrete mixer was to be attended. Two or three German civilians were in charge. They told everybody what to do and determined what quantity of cement, sand, gravel, and water had to be dumped into the rotating mouth of the mixer. We were shoveling sand and gravel or carrying bags of cement. Other Häftlinge had to push wheelbarrows full of concrete, and others spread out the concrete with shovels. All this work was hard, exhausting, and demanded considerable physical strength, which we were lacking. Persuasions, shouting, and whips by supervisors and that of the Vorarbeiter did not help much. We simply could not perform, as did usual workers. Therefore, one bag of cement (ninety pounds) had to be carried by two of us. And for many, even this was too much. We could throw into the mixer only half-full shovels of sand or gravel, and we could push a wheelbarrow filled with concrete to only one-third of its capacity. All this irritated the Germans, but after several guys collapsed and had to be removed from the work detail, they had no choice but to accept our efficiency as it was.

The work was progressing at half the speed with twice as many workers as it would be in normal circumstances. The German professional masters, as cruel and demanding as they were, told the SS officers over and over that if they wanted the work to be done, they had to give workers more food and more rest. But instead, the SS brought in more prisoners while, at the same time, our numbers were shrinking rapidly. At the end of our first day of "normal" work, we had to carry one dead and one sick to the Appell. And the next day was no better.

That first Sunday the roll call was outside the tunnels and in the fresh air. The weather was dark and misty, but to us, it appeared to be unbelievably bright. And the air without dust was intoxicating. Many became dizzy. This roll call was by Kommando to review our numbers and condition. It was not good! In this first week of living and working underground, 10 percent of us (twenty, to be exact) were gone. The rest of us were either Muselman, sick, or looking bad. However, our Kapo gave a speech, from which I understood only the following: (a) We were lazy bastards, and the efficiency of our work must increase; otherwise, he would ask the camp superior to transfer those disobedient to worse Kommandos. And (b) our Kommando was a very good one, and he treated us as a father treats his children. To appreciate this, he said we should inquire how it was in those Kommandos working where the tunnels were being cut out of the rock.

On this second count, he certainly was right. Losses over there were up to 10 percent daily—in particular among guys operating the pneumatic hammers. A hungry and weak man shocked by this devilish machine could not last longer than two days if forced to do this work all day. Sadistically, with cynicism and perfidy, the Germans assigned every Italian who showed up in Dora to this work. That was their bloody revenge for General Badoglio's switching to the Allied side. Yet they kept saying that Italians were famous for their stone-cutting skills and that was the reason why they were in the front row of tunnel cutters in Dora. Russians, for a change, famous as weight lifters, worked in the second row, loading rocks into wheelbarrows, rail carts, or conveyors. There are probably some records on how many prisoners have died in Dora. Whatever this figure is (probably between ten thousand or twenty thousand), in my opinion, 80 percent of them died during the construction of the tunnels between September 1943 and April 1944.

Sundays were also the days of changing shifts. Those who had been working from midnight to noon did not work for twenty-four hours, starting a new shift at noon on Monday. Those who worked from noon to midnight also did not work for twenty-four hours, starting work at 0000 (midnight) hour on Monday. Within these twenty-four hours, besides three Appells, the conventional distribution of food, and the fighting for beds, there were attempts to give us a possibility to clean ourselves. We were able to spend more time in the lavatory, where one faucet with cold water served fifty to one hundred men.

We could also exchange parts of our uniforms if some of them were worn out. Seldom did anyone want to take advantage of this opportunity; 90 percent preferred to rest, provided that a place to sit or lie down could be found. On Mondays, as a general rule, our Kommando was supplemented by a new Zugang. They always attempted to maintain about two hundred Häftlinge in Beton Kommando II. Kapo Hans, however, was always manipulating to keep our number at about 190. The reason for this was to have ten liters of soup extra for himself and for his Vorarbeiter. This was possible because the kettles or barrels in which the soup was sent out from the kitchen were all of the same size—thirteen gallons each. Our Kommando always got four barrels. Whenever the Arbeitsstatistik sent too many supplemental Häftlinge, it was a problem. If Hans did not succeed in getting rid of the surplus, we received less soup. The new prisoners supplementing our ranks were Russians, Gypsies, French, and Hungarian Jews, so our Kommando, originally almost exclusively Polish, became international.

Our Kapo was a German, but his red triangle indicated that he was a "political prisoner." I could talk to him. Since I forced myself to learn a few German words even before imprisonment, I understood about a third of what he was saying, and I said to him a few times, "*Guten Morgen*," or, "*Wie geht's Ihnen?*" This caused him to treat me a bit better than the others. For instance, when filling my messtin with soup, he would ladle out from the bottom of the barrel to get some heavier ingredients. I was also often ordered to move the empty barrels to tunnel B after the distribution of the soup. This was a privilege because I would scrape out whatever was left in the barrels. Such little extras meant a lot since our diet was way below the survival minimum.

Another privilege that I enjoyed was the occasional assignment to a less exhausting job such as chiseling out trenches for pipes or conduits in the rock subfloor. We did this using chisels, hammers, and pickaxes. This work would have been extremely hard and harmful to our hands if it were performed under constant supervision. But usually, two to four of us were left alone in one Halle. We did only enough to show some progress, then we would stand back-to-back, watching the opposite ends of the Halle for the approaching controller. We also made some noise by hitting our tools against stone. Otherwise, we kept talking for hours and hours, talking about ourselves, our families, politics, and war. But mostly this conversation was about food. A hungry man thinks and talks only about food. If we could have recorded all those gourmet dreams of ours, it could become an impressive cookbook.

Unfortunately, my friend Władek was not given the trench-cutting work nor the heavier soup, and he was deteriorating faster than I. He was already almost a Muselman when a disaster hit me. I fell sick with fever, diarrhea, and terrible headaches, which kept me down for three days. Then an enormous ulcer grew on my neck, under my chin. It was as if the rest of my substance was assembling in this abscess. The pain grew with its size. Moving my head was out of the question. Any movement, for that matter, increased the pain. I was in such bad shape that they let me stay on the block, not working. I could demand to be sent to the camp hospital, but any conscious Häftling avoided that. In Birkenau and in the early months in Dora, we did not see anyone come out of the hospital healed. So I suffered alone in this huge underground dormitory, lying on the top level of one of the racks.

Looking up from the bed, racked with pain, I would see the rocky texture of the tunnel arching above me and the few electric bulbs fading off in the distance beyond the ever-present dust. It was a far cry from the blue sky, which I had marveled at when roaming the fields and meadows in my youth. I prayed to God Almighty to cut short this misery of mine and take my soul into His custody, somewhere beyond that sky. But this was not His intention. Instead, He sent me to the latrine. And those in the tunnels were nothing more than large steel containers about three feet in diameter and some sixteen inches high called *kibel* (Polish for *bucket*). I had to walk a long distance to find one. Władek or someone else provided me with a piece of board, which I used as a walking stick. After finally finding a stinking container, I put my board on the rim to have something to sit on, and at the last moment, I dropped my pants and sat down. It was a tremendous relief, but it also made me terribly weak. I could not get up. I did not want to get up. I was just sitting there with that ulcer, now the size of a large orange, pulling me down, down, down… I almost fell backward into that horrible, stinking mess when someone jerked on my shoulder. "Get out of here, you stinking Muselman." That was the "kibel Kommando," whose job it was to empty those containers.

When I picked myself up, the man noticed the enormous red-blue-and-white ulcer on my neck. He said, "You, go about fifty steps that way and around that corner, and you'll find a doctor there." I did so using my last ounce of energy.

In a small wooden shanty with one door, one window, a table, a chair, and a cabinet, a man was providing some medical assistance. He was a young Russian, tall and jovial—a paramedic, I hoped. He glanced at me and exclaimed in Russian, "God have mercy, what a monstrosity you have!" He told me that he had never seen an abscess so big and so infected. He went on to say that it looked like a hopeless case but that if I wanted, he could cut it with no promise that I would survive this operation. Without hesitating, I said, "Cut!" He found a small primitive kitchen knife with a wooden handle and sharpened it on a piece of leather belt. Then he lit a kerosene lamp and held the blade in the flame for a while. He ordered me to sit down on the chair and hold a tin bowl under my ulcer. While still talking about something, without a warning, he made the cut.

The pain in that second was indescribable. I fainted, but the skilled medic had dropped his knife and, with one hand, grabbed the bowl. With the other, he held me by the collar of my jacket. After the pus and blood stopped running, he lowered me to the floor, washed the wound with some kind of disinfectant, wrapped my neck with a paper bandage, and gave me some pills. There was drinking water in the first aid shanty, so I drank a lot.

The medic said, "*Khrabryy paren. Siychas ukhodi. Priyti zavtra*" (Brave lad, get out now and come back tomorrow). I felt much, much better without that poison in the abscess and with clear water in my belly. I had kept my bread from the two previous days in my messtin and in my pockets, and now I was able to eat it. Fortunately, the Kapo decided that I did not have to work for at least one more day. So I saw my Russian doctor for a second time. He changed bandages, gave me another pill and water, and said, "It looks better. You may survive." And so with the help of the heavier soup and trench-cutting assignments, I began regaining my strength. In no time, I was again in better physical condition than Władek.

On the Sunday before Christmas, as usual the Appell was outside of the tunnels. The air temperature was now lower than in the tunnels. The mud was frozen and resembled how it was in Birkenau. We thought of how good it was to be in the tunnels! However, it was not so good at all. During this roll call, it became clear that from the two hundred prisoners who arrived from Buchenwald on November 2, only twenty-two remained. And this was a "better" Kommando.

In 1943, there was no Christmas for me or anyone in the tunnels of Dora. We did not even realize what day it was. The work was as usual, the fight for survival was as usual, and there was just a glimmer of hope, as usual. Nevertheless, this slight glimmer was important to keep us going.

Building the camp

I am not sure if this was before New Year's or after when a sudden change in my wretched existence occurred. One morning, shortly after the distribution of soup at 6:00 a.m., a messenger from the Arbeitsstatistik arrived, and the Kapo ordered our Kommando to assemble in formation. His announcement was short: an order arrived that ten Häftlinge from this Kommando must be transferred to the Kommando called the *Transport Kolonne*. We grew numb. Everybody knew that this was equal to a death sentence. This was worse than loading the carts with rocks in the newly built tunnels. Transport Kolonne was working outside, carrying all kind of goods to a variety of destinations. They would be unloading railroad cars and highway trucks, hauling materials and equipment for the camp and for the future assembly plant. All this was done in a big hurry and under the direct supervision of SS men. Our kapo selected who would go. Those whom he disliked and the Muselmanen were good for nothing, in his opinion. Halfway through his selections, he pointed out my friend Władek Ptak. Władek resigned, grabbed my hand, and shook it without a word and with tears in his eyes as if saying good-bye forever. I couldn't stand it. I stepped out together with Władek and said, "Kapo Hans, please do not send him out! He is my friend!"

Kapo Hans answered, "So what? He is going to die in a day or two anyway. I don't need him. He has to go."

Impulsively I said, "If so, I am going with him."

Kapo Hans answered, "You know this is up to me, but if you insist, go."

And so it happened! We both left Beton Kommando II for the infamous Transport Kolonne.

Under the leadership of the fellow from the Arbeitsstatistik, the ten of us marched through tunnel B down to and through the well-guarded entry and exit gate. When exiting, the reporting ceremony was more complex than when entering. It had to be explained where we were going and why. Our numbers were written down by an SS officer. Then we went to the Arbeitsstatistik office. We stood outside, waiting for some formalities to be concluded. Finally, the Vorarbeiter from Transport Kolonne arrived: a rough-looking Soviet of Asiatic origin. He drove us toward the long line of boxcars being unloaded. Here, hundreds of Häftlinge were moving like ants along a dead snake. The air was filled with snow mixed with rain and mist but also with the noise of a multitude of shouts. Groups of Häftlinge, lifting heavy objects together, were counting in unison: "One, two, three—hoop!" Vorarbeiter were shouting orders about what to do or how to do it. Working men were screaming to each other, "Help! Take it! Move!" All these shouts in different languages were dominated by the German "*Los! Schnell!*" shouted by SS men, intermingled with barking guard dogs.

They made us carry narrow rail-gauge assemblies (two rails about two feet apart, already mounted on their steel ties). Such an assembly, about twenty to twenty-five feet long, could be probably lifted by six or eight men in normal physical condition. But twenty run-down, beaten prisoners could barely move it. With ten or twelve on each side, we had to grab ice-cold steel with our bare hands and carry it from the railroad car to a storage area some 150 steps away. The synchronization of our steps was particularly difficult since the ground was uneven, full of holes and hills covered with water mixed with broken ice.

If a fellow in a row of carriers tripped and fell, he remained there in the mud, trampled by those behind him. If a few of them fell, simultaneously they pulled down the rails and crushed the rest of the guys on the same side of the carried rail assembly. Of course, the sticks of the Vorarbeiter, the whips or rifle butts of the SS men, or the fangs of the German shepherd guard dogs helped very little to have the entire gang—or what was left of them—back on their feet and get them moving. And many with broken bones or overcome with exhaustion did not get up whatsoever.

I did not know (and I do not know now) how it was possible that nothing happened to me during this macabre work. Władek was behind me when we lugged the first rail assembly. When it became obvious that he was of no help at the rails, they had him carry some smaller items, but even that totally wore him out. Fortunately, it was a short workday for us as we started work at about noon, and by three or four, it was too dark to continue. We collected the sick and dead and lined up in the formal "*zu fünf*" formation. SS officers counted us, and after confirming the numbers with the Arbeitsstatistik, they ordered us to pile up the dead corpses in one spot and to take the sick to the "Hospital". Władek was sick and weak, and he was leaning against me. However, he did not want to go to this infirmary in a tent surrounded with mud. A few comrades helped me, and we succeeded to get him back into the tunnels. We had to now sleep in a different block where all Kommandos working outside were accommodated.

Due to some administrative error, during this change of Kommandos and Blocks, we got an extra ration of soup and bread. Also, despite the usually long roll calls, we had much more time for rest and sleep. All this was very important to build up our strength, and the result was that, the next morning, my poor Władek could walk without assistance and went out to work with our detail. This time our job was to unload bricks from the railroad platform. We formed a long line, and the bricks were passed from man to man. It was much easier and safer than carrying the rails. However, there were two problems: (1) our feet were freezing from being buried in mud up to our ankles, and (2) worse, our unprotected hands were terribly abused by the icy steel of yesterday and by porous bricks today. There were a few lucky guys who had gloves. I made my mind up to ask for some from a Vorarbeiter, Kapo, or even an SS man, should I notice any of them in an accessible mood. In the meantime, I tried to protect my hands with rags or paper from cement bags. We were unloading one platform of bricks for three hours.

When this was finished, some of us were ordered to arrange the bricks in neat rectangular stacks. Others had to unload some boards. Suddenly, at about noon, we heard strident whistles, upon which the Kapo and Vorarbeiter started to shout: *"Antreten! Antreten!"* (Get into the file!) and led us to a dryer spot within the big railroad yard where we were working. They lined us up in a double row, not the usual five rows deep. A group of SS officers (perhaps five or six) approached, and one of them said, "We want to verify your professional skills." A lightning of hope struck my mind. Instinctively I knew that they needed people for the assembly plant being installed in the completed tunnels. I said to Władek and two other Polish fellows standing nearby, "Let's say we are mechanics."

Someone said, "What kind of mechanics? Let's be specific."

Then added, "I am an auto mechanic."

The other one said, "I am a locksmith."

Władek said, "I do not know any work like this. What shall I say?"

Somebody suggested, "Call yourself an electrician."

"Okay," I said, "I'll call myself a sheet metal worker."

Now we started to worry. What if they checked our records? They would find something else. For instance, I had been recorded by the Gestapo and everywhere else as a forester. They might punish us. But how? We were already at the end of the line, and it was only a matter of days till we died. So let's take a chance.

In the meantime, the SS men started from both ends of our double row, asking each one for his number and profession. Sometimes they asked specifics: "What did you actually do as such?" Finally, they came to us. We told them what we decided to say. After they had recorded everybody, the lists were submitted to an *Obersturmführer* (lieutenant), who made some notations on them. With this completed, he turned to us and said, "The number I will read, step out." He called out about thirty Häftlinge, among them all four of us. "*Antreten zu zwei! Achtung! Rechts um! Marsch!*" We were led to the tunnel entrance. Here they wrote down our numbers again and ordered us to go to Halle 20 and report to the Kapo of Savatzki Kommando. That we did, but the Kapo was not there. His Schreiber did not know what this was all about and decided to ask Kapos or Vorarbeiter on various Hallen whether they needed some extra men. Some of them confirmed that they did and arrived in no time to pick out whom they liked. In most cases, the right answers to some professional questions decided whom we went with. So four of them took twenty of our group. Among them was our Polish auto mechanic. That left ten of us. The Savatzki Kommando Schreiber suggested that we should go to several Hallen where no Vorarbeiter answered the phone. Perhaps they would take us. So we walked from Halle to Halle, but only one out of ten of us were engaged because, by chance, he met a friend who was already working there. This friend asked a German civilian supervisor, who said, "Okay, let him stay."

Nine of us remained "unemployed"—a situation without precedent in concentration camps. It was nice to do nothing for a while—in particular to be away from Transport Kolonne. I had never been so far in the tunnels. As far as I remember, we reached Halle number 8. All these cross tunnels from number 19 on down were already converted into assembly plant departments, all clean, free of dust, supplied with conditioned air, furnished with sophisticated equipment and tools. What a pity that there was no room for us in that working paradise.

We found a niche in the west wall of tunnel B, somewhere opposite Halle 22, and there we remained resting for the remainder of the day. We discussed among ourselves what we should do. Our group of lost souls consisted of one Belgian, one Czech, one German, three Poles, and three Soviets. The German and Czech were of the opinion that we must immediately report to SS authorities and clarify the situation while the Russians were opposing this idea but had no alternative to offer. The Poles and the Belgian suggested to stay where we were until the time when the outdoor Kommandos started coming for the Appell to the dormitory block. We speculated that we might join them to receive our food rations and get a night of sleep. We were also hoping that next morning, the Savatzki Kommando would employ us.

Everything worked fine except the last one. Savatzki Kommando did not want us. The prospect of losing our daily soup and being disciplined for not reporting and that we were not attached to any Kommando forced us to make a dramatic decision. We decided to report to the Arbeitsstatistik office. Reluctant and with anxiety, we walked slowly to the south exit of tunnel B. Our prime concern was how to avoid being sent back to Transport Kolonne. This was a real possibility because where could they send us if the Savatzki people said that they did not need more help? Shortly before reaching the gate, we elected our German fellow prisoner to be the leader of our group and report to the guard on duty why and where we were going and give him our numbers. With this accomplished, we found ourselves in no time at the entrance to the Arbeitsstatistik. We lost the courage to knock on the door. Undecided, we stood in the muddy square, some distance away from the office entrance. The office appeared to be very busy. SS officers, Blockältester, and Kapos were entering and leaving. Suddenly I noticed a distinctive-looking prisoner approaching the office entrance. He was a tall fellow in the stripped Häftling uniform but clean and well fitted. The armband on his right sleeve with the inscription "Lager Dolmetscher" indicated that he was a camp interpreter. A bright-red triangle with the letter *P* indicated that he was a Pole, and his face and manner suggested that he was an intelligent man. Instinctively I approached him and said in Polish, "Comrade, I and these fellows behind me are in a peculiar and critical situation. Can you help us?"

He turned his head in surprise and asked, "Who are you people? What is the matter?" I briefly told him our story, after which he exclaimed, "Unbelievable! But let me see what we can do!" He entered the office and, after maybe fifteen minutes, came out with the Kapo of the Arbeitsstatistik. This Kapo had a red triangle without a letter, meaning he was a German. But he spoke fluent Polish. I had to tell him our story again with more details. He asked a few of the other guys in our group related questions and recorded our numbers and professions.

At this time, I shall mention that much later, I learned the names of these two men who in fact saved my life. The interpreter's name was Tadeusz Pacer, and the Kapo of the Arbeitsstatistik was Jan Kaczmarek. Remarkably, these are the only two names of the thousands of my coprisoners that I can remember in full except, of course, my friends, whom I knew before arrest—J. Kuhn and W. Ptak—and that of Stanisław Lipinski, with whom I was liberated. A few other persons I do remember by their first names, even fewer by their last names only.

It was obvious that these two men did not believe that I was a sheet metal worker and Władek an electrician, but they recorded it as given and disappeared into the office. Soon thereafter, two messengers left the office in a hurry, and almost one hour later, several Kapos arrived. They entered the Arbeitsstatistik, and the nine of us remained standing in the cold and freezing mist, trembling with cold, hunger, and anxiety. Then three Kapos came out of the office, all of them Czech, all with unhappy faces and pieces of paper in their hands. Each read three of our numbers and ordered us to follow him. Władek, one "Russian," and I were taken by a fellow who looked the least intelligent of the three but certainly the most humane. He led us through the new camp construction site to a semifinished barracks used as a workshop and storage for his Kommando. It was *Ofensetzer* Kommando, which means "Stove Installers Command." The remainder of the guys who shared our "unemployment" predicament were assigned as follows: three to the locksmith and three to the plumbing Kommando. When we entered the Ofensetzer's barracks, four or five Häftlinge were busy with something in the workshop. The Kapo said to them in Czech what I understood as more or less, "Arbeitsstatistik forced me to take three new guys, so give them something to eat." What a heavenly surprise. The very first time in this new Kommando, without even working or waiting, we each got a full messtin of heavy, heavy soup. And so started our convalescence.

With our arrival, the Ofensetzer Kommando consisted of twenty-one men. The Kapo and seventeen other "specialists" all were Czechs. The new Zugang of three—in particular the two Poles—was not appreciated because this Kommando was a secure, true shelter for privileged prisoners. Almost all Kommandos building the new camp Dora outside of the tunnels were like this one. They were organized in Buchenwald and sent here for a particular purpose. Of the numerous advantages of being in such a Kommando was first and foremost the extra food. As mentioned before, the camp kitchen sent out soup only in thirteen-gallon barrels; therefore, a Kommando like this one received two or three times as much as most of the other prisoners were entitled to. Moreover, all the Czechs who had been in Buchenwald for a long time were receiving regularly parcels from their families, friends, or organizations. Many of these parcels contained elaborate food products or raw ingredients. So all eighteen of our comrades rarely ate the camp soup. Sometimes they would prepare fancy dishes for themselves in the workshop. I noticed that the Kapo was the poorest of them all, so every day, another one of his subordinates shared with him his meal, which was prepared from his own ingredients. Sometimes they all contributed something and prepared a common meal. Once in a while, even we were invited to the feast. Anyway, after one hundred days of hunger and misery, we now began one hundred days of plenty—plenty of soup at least.

Another advantage in our new Kommando was—more sleep! Our daily routine was more normal and better organized. We worked during the daytime and slept at night. In the block, we always occupied the same beds, had the same blankets, and even had a cushion, provided you could get one. The distribution of bread did not require any ceremonies and took a short time, only the roll calls were as usual, a nuisance mainly because the transport Kolonne and some other "dirty" Kommandos caused trouble by delays and missing Häftling. Of course, the outdoor dust-free fresh air during our work hours was beneficial too. Unfortunately, the dust was still plentiful in the dormitory block. In any event, finally, our work was easy and not at all exhausting. Our job was to install iron stoves in the newly erected barracks.

Whenever a barrack was constructed by the carpenters Kommando, we were usually the first in to start with the installation of the stoves. After us, the electricians, plumbers, locksmiths, and painters moved in. A typical dormitory barrack in Dora consisted of a vestibule that led to a large dining area, behind which were large "bedrooms." There were about 120 beds in each bedroom, forty units of three levels each. From the same vestibule, one also entered two small rooms, one of which was the lavatory while the other the toilet. We had to furnish all six of these rooms with stoves—four larger ones and two smaller. In predetermined locations, we had to cut out oversized openings for the stove pipes. On the top of the roof and on the bottom of the ceiling, we attached a sheet metal cone, through which the stove pipe was fitted—the pipe that runs from the top or side of each stove. After making everything tight with asbestos wool, the stove could be used for heating the space.

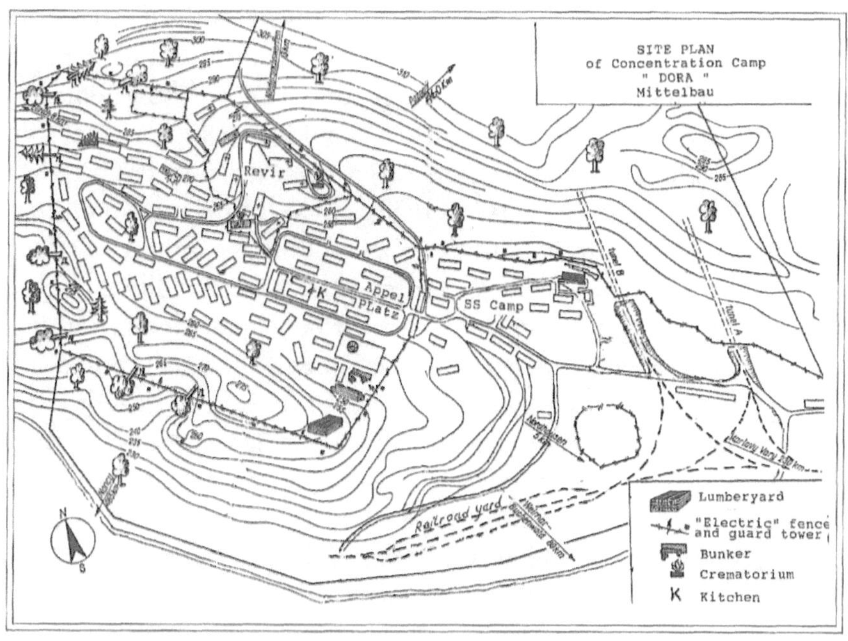

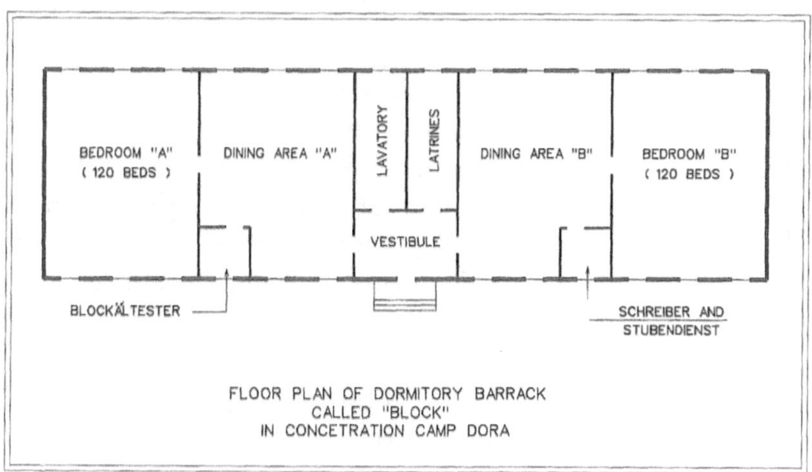

Do not think that we had to carry those heavy cast-iron stoves. Oh, no! This was the job of the Transport Kolonne. The selfishness of workers' unions was strictly enforced in the concentration camp. We were even prohibited to help Muselmanen struggling with clumsiness and exhaustion when carrying any bulky and substantial load. What a lack of justice and outright cruelty—healthy and strong men just waiting and watching dying skeletons hauling those materials that were needed! We worked without any kind of supervision. Our Kapo just told us which barrack to go to and when it was ready for us. Of course, at least twice daily, an SS inspector would visit each work area, but it would be just a few minutes of him watching us working. Then he proceeded to another barrack. All we had to do was pay appropriate attention not to be caught doing nothing. Usually, we hurriedly erected a stove in one of the small rooms (the lavatory or toilet) to have a warm place to sit in. One of us kept guard and watched for the approaching inspector whereas the other three would rest by the warm stove. Occasionally, we permitted fellows from the other trades or even those from the Transport Kolonne to warm up by our stove. However, it was a dangerous precedent, and the experienced Czechs warned us not to do so. Sometimes the SS men would show up suddenly, and the signal by the watchman was just in time to alert us to start pounding a piece of steel or start cutting some sheet metal. A Häftling from any other Kommando found in our warm "workroom" or running out of there could be a disaster not only for himself but for us as well. Unfortunately, there were also cases of treason or denunciations by undercover agents recruited among the prisoners by perfidious SS officers for a pack of cigarettes or some privilege. Anyone found guilty of "sabotage of work" by willfully not working or allowing others not to work were punished by being sent to the *Strafe* Kommando, which was a penalty work detachment. Despite all such rigors and other time controlling measures, we were able to find hundreds of reasons and excuses why the work was not progressing. The result was that it took a week or ten days to install those six stoves. Under normal conditions, a four-man crew could do this in one day.

These three months, or one hundred days, with "Ofensetzer" were really good for us. We gained weight, strength, and health. In particular, Władek had come back to his original physical condition and good spirit. It certainly helped him survive the horrors of these concentration camps. Our only discord on that Kommando was the cool relationship between the two of us and our Czech comrades. They simply did not like us since we were Poles. In their opinion, Poles were bad because nine hundred years ago, a Polish king invaded their homeland, and then five hundred years later, the Poles drove a Czech king's army out of Silesia; because one hundred years ago, the Pan-Slavic ideology, so popular among the Czech, was not embraced by Poles; because twenty years ago, Poland defeated Soviet Russia; because five years ago, when Hitler was dismantling Czechoslovakia, Polish forces occupied 385 square miles of Czech territory; and so on. The Czechs were much friendlier to the Soviet man who arrived with us. However, when it became known that he was Ukrainian with nationalistic inclinations, they cooled off toward him as well. If not for political motivations, the Czechs were good comrades and easygoing fellows. We even learned a few Czech songs from them.

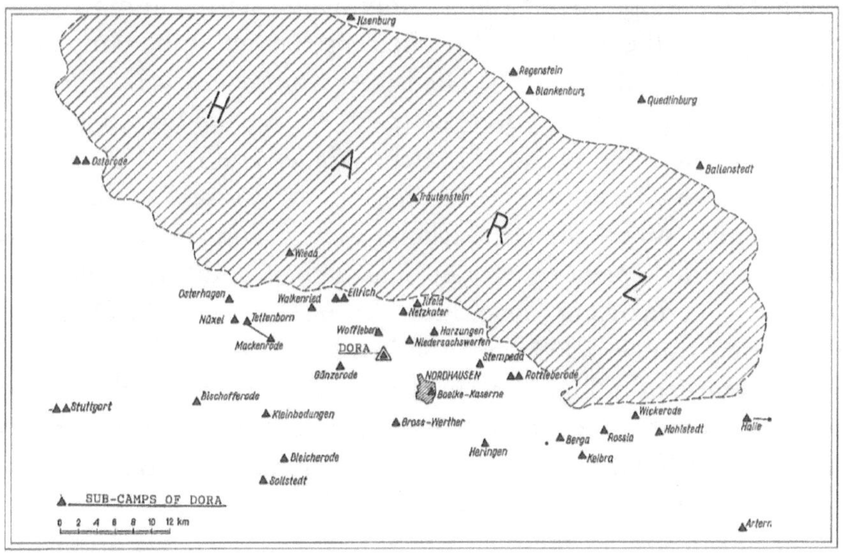

CHAPTER 8

In an *Außenkommando*

By March 1944, there were enough barracks completed that all Kommandos working outside of the tunnels could be accommodated in them. Also, the kitchen and administrative barracks were completed. In April, the Savatzki Kommando started to move from the tunnels to the new barracks. The construction of the camp facilities was nearing the end. The Ofensetzer Kommando was in danger. Gradually they started to decrease it. Of course, the first to go were the last arrivals. By the end of March, Władek and I, the Ukrainian, and even two Czechs got the transfer order. I was sent to the *Außen* Kommando. Where the other fellows went, I don't remember. This was a dreadful happening because Władek Ptak and I were separated just about permanently! I ran into him once or twice in Dora and then a final time in 1968 when I visited him in Kraków.

Before continuing my personal story, I have to clarify the general development of the concentration camp Mittelbau I, called Dora. As mentioned before, it was one of many subcamps of Buchenwald. However, it was, as a facility, growing rapidly in the number of prisoners and in size. In the first half of the year 1944, the drilling of tunnels was completed, and in the entire underground system, a V-2 rocket assembly plant was established. At the same time, the barracks for the prisoners and for the SS troops were also completed, so by the end of May 1944, nobody was living in the tunnels. Also, at the same time, many similar subcamps were set up wherever workers were needed. Buchenwald organized these subcamps such as Dora directly or as a sub-subcamp managed by Dora. The number of subcamps spread out around Dora in a radius of about ten miles. However, the city of Nordhausen, with many workshops and factories, was only 3.5 miles away from the camp Dora, so the SS command decided to supply this city's industry with manpower directly from the main camp. The group of prisoners working in the many different shops in Nordhausen was called the Außen Kommando. It existed from March 1944 until January 10, 1945. During the summer of 1944, it averaged 150 prisoners employed in ten different facilities. Usually, two trucks would haul these men into the city in the morning and back to the camp in the evening. In the autumn of 1944, the number of prisoners in Dora exceeded thirty thousand, and Mittelbau I became independent from Buchenwald, a self-administered, major concentration camp with at least thirty subcamps.

Apparently, the SS organization was well paid by the Nordhausen industry for the manpower supplied because they paid particular attention to the selection of prisoners to the Außen Kommandos. We were assigned to each plant individually by the Arbeitsstatistik then reviewed by the eighty-eight officers who dealt with the plant managers. I do not remember if there was a Kapo for this Kommando.

I was told by a clerk from the Arbeitsstatistik to report to a particular area of the Appellplatz where the Außen Kommando assembled immediately after the morning roll call. I and a few other new members of the Kommando were presented to the Obersturmführer in charge, who accepted all of us. Then each of us was told where we would work. My assignment was at Niemeier Vulcanization Werke. So I joined a group of ten Häftlinge, one of whom was holding a sign on a stick with the name of the shop. Our marching formation was as usual—five in a row; however, each sub-Kommando (or shop) would march separate from the others by at least two steps. SubKommandos were of different sizes, from forty in the *Fleischerei* (meat processing plant) to five in the Waescherei (laundry).

Each truck would carry laborers to four or five plants. Those who were going furthest had to board first, and those, who disembarked first, had to board last. We were obliged to march in this order to avoid a mix-up at the trucks. Whoever marched at the right end of the first row of five would carry our sign facing to the right so that the SS man controlling our passage through the gate could read it easily. He also counted us and recorded the number. And we marched past him as usual with caps off and our hands motionless at the seams of our pants. We packed in deep under the canvas top of the truck. Near the tailgate of the truck were a couple of benches for the SS guards, two for each plant or shop. I think that the Fleischerei Kommando needed four guards. The ride took ten to fifteen minutes. We were the second to disembark. Sometimes, however, they let us out of the truck all in the same spot, then we had to walk two or three blocks to our shop.

The vulcanization shop of Mr. Niemeier was a medium-sized facility. It occupied a city lot, narrow but very deep. In the front portion of the building, facing the street, were a few offices. There was the shop proper and a warehouse in the rear. Next to the shop, in a lean-to, there was the boiler. There was a small side yard at the front of the building and another small yard at the rear of the boiler lean-to. It was through these yards that we entered the shop and boiler room and where the SS guards kept their watch. All other openings to the workshop were securely locked.

Herr Niemeier ran his business himself. He was about sixty years old and employed two secretaries in his office. In the shop, there were four German *Meisters* as well as two French and two Byelorussian civilian workers. The rest of the crew consisted of us, the prisoners or slaves of the XX century. Our number varied depending on work volume. However, most of the time, there were nine of us: one Austrian, imprisoned for being a homosexual; one Belgian, arrested for listening to BBC; one German, an inmate already for twenty years, sentenced to life for killing a policeman; one Pole, me; four Soviets, fugitives from a prisoner of war camp; and one Czech, a peasant who refused to go to work in Germany "voluntarily." The German and Austrian would attend to the boiler. The rest of us worked in the shop, repairing worn-out tires.

I think that anybody can be a vulcanizer, provided he had the equipment and materials necessary for this work. It was a simple procedure. One had to remove old, damaged rubber as much as possible down to the thread reinforcement of the tire then, using the appropriate adhesive system, apply a new cover with a layer of soft raw rubber. Then one had to put the tire, with the inner tube inside, into the iron form, which served as a pressure cooker. By filling the inner tube with compressed air, it pressed the raw rubber against the tread-forming pattern of the form. Then, by injecting steam into the coil system surrounding the form, the new rubber would get cooked, so it became hard. A bit more sophisticated work was needed with blown tires, where the torn thread reinforcement would need to be repaired or partially replaced. My job was to grind off old rubber and apply new rubber. It would be boring to describe our work in this shop in detail, day in and day out.

More interesting, however, were other aspects of our life in those days. The four Soviets and the German were the first Häftlinge employed by Niemeier. Everybody else joined later. I do not remember if anyone of this group was officially named a Vorarbeiter nor that plant management bestowed any authority or privileges on any of us. If it was necessary to speak for our group, it was natural that the German, whose first name was Hans, or the Austrian would do so. However, Nicolai, one of the Soviet men who spoke German well, felt he should. Consequently, Hans and Nicolai developed a bitter rivalry whereby Nicolai counted on internal support, having majority on his side (three other Soviets and one Czech) whereas the German, relying on external power, counted on his affiliation to the superior race. In the end, Nicolai prevailed. He was by far a more intelligent and educated individual. Unfortunately, he was also a dedicated communist and party member, and as such, he kept the other three Soviets in check. Of these four, Nicolai and Misha were Ukrainians from Kiev or its vicinity whereas Sasha and Alosha were Byelorussians from the eastern part of that country. All four were well built and strong men.

Influenced by Nicolai, the Soviet prisoners considered the two civilian Byelorussians as traitors of the Soviet Union, unworthy of friendly relationships. Secretly, however, they did have some business together. When I joined the Niemeier Kommando, all four Soviets were, for at least the first month, extremely cool toward me. I spoke enough Russian and Ukrainian to communicate with them without much difficulty. Yet they kept their distance, avoiding any conversations with me except for necessary exchanges of information related strictly with our daily life at work. One day I told them that the Polish army was fighting in Italy. One of them exclaimed, *"Kakoy ty Polyak? Ty Zapadnyy!"* This means, "What kind of Pole are you? You are Western Ukrainian!" That opened my eyes. They had considered me to be a Ukrainian from the territory that used to be within the borders of Poland before WWII. And in their opinion, all of those Ukrainians were extreme nationalists cooperating with the Germans. It took me a long time to convince them that they were wrong and that despite the fact that I lived in that territory, I was a Pole and nothing else. This broke the ice, and our relationship improved considerably.

Of course, we disagreed on many points—in particular the subject of communist ideology and the many facts from history that were presented to them in Soviet schools in a twisted manner. Nicolai was quite aggressive in our discussions, but his three pals paid more attention to my arguments. And I am sure that their belief in his dogma was weakened. However, the majority of our half-hour lunch breaks I spent with the Belgian boy (he was three or four years younger than I) and the two civilian Frenchmen. Even though it was prohibited to communicate with civilians, the SS guard seldom interfered. Such an attitude was, on one hand, logical because there was no way for them to prevent our conversations during work time and, on another hand, practical because they knew that we, the prisoners, could cause a lot of difficulties for the guards if we wanted to. Therefore, it was better for them to leave us alone. The French guys were pretty amusing. Both were factory workers with just primary education, but they were intelligent men, always joking instead of swearing or complaining. I could hardly understand them, but the Belgian translated the slang into a more literary language. Most curious was their physical appearance. Both were skinny, but one was tall with a head full of dark curly hair, the other short, always with a black cap on his head and a cigarette hanging from his lips. Clad in black overalls, they looked like miserable weaklings. Nevertheless, my conversations with those three French-speaking men improved my French considerably.

The first few weeks in this new Kommando meant I would be hungry again. In the newly built camp outside the tunnels, all food was received in your block. No more soup for the Kommando. Also, it was not necessary that the entire Kommando should sleep in the same block. Somehow, I found myself living in block number 25, where only a few other members of the Außen Kommando were accommodated. The rest of us were spread out in many other blocks. My Blockältester was a cruel man called Max. He not only treated his subjects harshly but also unceremoniously robbed them of their meager food rations. Anyway, it was back to camp food without any extras. Taking into consideration all the "losses" during transport, in warehouses, in the kitchen, and in distribution, I received probably 800 calories of the 1,100 officially supplied by authorities per each inmate. Kindly note that an efficiently working man needs 2,000 to 2,500 calories under normal conditions. I was as hungry as the Belgian fellow. However, the other prisoners working in Niemeier's shop did not appear to be so hungry. I wondered where they got all the extra bread and margarine, which they ate during lunch—in particular the Soviet men who did not receive any help from their homes. For a long time, that remained their secret. Luckily, in April, my provisions improved suddenly and considerably. Parcels from my foster parents, from other family members, and even from Mr. and Mrs. Kuhn (Jurek's parents) arrived. Three parcels arrived before any letter announcing them. Therefore, it was quite a surprise to be called to the camp post office to collect those parcels.

The post office was located in one of the barracks that had its own entrance gate. I had to open my parcels in the presence of an SS man who carefully inspected the contents. In this case, he did not confiscate anything, so I brought everything to my block. Oh! Dear Lord! What an abundance—smoked meat and pork fat, canned meat, high-protein bread, sugar, chocolate, and, above all, onion and garlic. There were also socks, gloves, a sweater, underwear, and—wow!—shoes. The two items I appreciated most were the onion and the shoes. It was unbelievable how devoid my body system was of vitamins and other natural ingredients. So despite me disliking onions in the past even avoiding dishes that smelled of onion, this onion tasted like a heavenly delicacy. And of course, those were the best shoes of my life.

After seven months of wearing wooden camp clogs, I felt like a king in the new, solid, comfortable, ankle-high type leather shoes. I succeeded in preserving them until the last days of my detention; however, it was not a simple matter.

In general, there was a considerable problem how to store, for even a few days, goods that one received in a parcel. An ordinary Häftling did not have any storage space of his own. All that one had was sixteen square feet of bed area. There was some space under the lowest bed; however, it was prohibited to store anything there. Using this space was a risk with a 95 percent chance of losing whatever one left there. It could be stolen or "confiscated" by the Stubendienst. There was the possibility to ask the Blockältester to keep it safe in his *Stube* (room or enclosed area). But that meant having to share with him your precious belongings. And sure enough, every day the Stubendienst prepared for their boss and themselves a fancy meal made with the ingredients "stored in their Stube." It was unavoidable not to pay your tribute to these bastards. So I had to do so also. However, I was in a more fortunate situation because I was able to take most of my goodies to the Niemeier shop and hide them there. Parcels and letters from the family were a big moral support and certainly helped my diet. However, for me they were irregular and short-lived. When the Soviet army entered Polish territory, the German postal service from there became very restricted. By far, what was more reliable and long-lasting was the illegal market in which I became involved.

The suggestion originated from my French civilian coworkers. They said one day to the Belgian and me, "Why don't you help yourself as the Russians do? We will provide you with tobacco, and you bring us bread and butter!" That was a revelation! It was dangerous and not the most ethical business; however, it solved most of our problems. How was this possible?

In the city of Nordhausen, there were several plants producing chewing tobacco. Many women and foreigners, some of them relatives of our French and Byelorussian comrades, worked in those plants. They would smuggle out tobacco leaves that were in various stages of curing. Their husbands, brothers, or boyfriends brought these leaves to our shop. We the prisoners, in turn, would smuggle this tobacco into the concentration camp, where it was a priceless commodity.

At this point, let me insert a few remarks on the subject of smoking in concentration camps. The habit or addiction was, for many, tragically strong. In general, it was not forbidden to smoke. There was even a time when we received a few cigarettes as part of our official daily rations. However, most of the time, there was no tobacco in the camp—period! A majority of the prisoners could live without it. For me, although I smoked before my arrest and always had the urge to smoke, I could get along without it if it was not available. But there were some people who would give anything for a smoke. Starving of hunger, they were ready to give a piece of bread or a bowl of soup for a cigarette. Freezing in bitter cold, they would give their shoes or a jacket for that bloody tobacco. And there were others for whom smoking was not only a pleasure but also a proof of superiority. Those, while smoking, apparently felt stronger, smarter, and even entitled. I did not deal with the poor unrestrained addicts. My clients were the fellows working in the kitchen, in the *Versorgung* Kommando (supply), and in the *Kleiderkammer* Kommando (clothing).

Many Poles worked in the kitchen and supply Kommandos whereas in the clothing warehouse, it was mostly Jews. The wealthiest were the guys from the Versorgung Kommando. They brought the food in from various warehouses and food processing plants. From them I got loaves of bread, bricks of margarine, and whole sausages. Business was risky but profitable. On each transaction, I made 100 percent profit. Having no possibility to accumulate any wealth, I simply limited the number of transactions to one or two per week. It was enough for me to not be hungry, make friends among influential personalities, and secure good and clean clothes for myself. The last was as much convenient and healthy as self-conceited.

The tailors in the clothing warehouse made a suit for me. It was also a striped prisoner's uniform but was of better fabric and had more lively colors. The stripes were a bit narrower and were still white and blue but without the standard grayish appearance. This suit fitted me so well that I looked sharp, clean, and better than many Blockältester, *Kapos*, or other camp higher-ups. Wearing my new shoes, which I polished with shoe polish purchased in Nordhausen, and that suit, which I managed to keep neat, I felt good and comfortable. Also, thanks to this better appearance, I received some fringe benefits.

Most important to me was the improved measure of respect and restraint given by many SS men and all the German civilians I had to deal with. On the other hand, however, it was quite a challenge to maintain such a distinct appearance, being nobody but a simple Häftling. For instance, I acquired another suit, which I used for work and kept at the Niemeier shop. The most difficult part, however, was saving my belongings from the disaster of Entlausung. This disinfecting procedure, aimed to kill lice, was conducted once each month. As usual, the entire block had to go to the bath facility. The Blockältester, with the help of the Stubendienst and Lagerschutz, made sure that everybody went. They also made sure everybody took with him all his clothing including their blanket. Only the straw-filled mattresses could remain on the beds. Before entering the bathhouse, you had to strip completely, putting your suit and cap in one container, underwear in the other one, and shoes in a separate pile. In the bathhouse, you were sprayed with a liquid soap having limited disinfecting value, then you walked through a row of showers. On the other end of the building, you received clean clothes. But they were not yours, which seldom fit you and required sewing on your number and triangle, which were ripped off the old ones. This procedure was later improved, so your clothes were disinfected in a steam bath while you were taking your shower, and they were dumped at the exit of the bathhouse. It took some time to find your things, but at least those were yours. Unfortunately, the steam applied to our uniforms perhaps killed some lice but did not wash anything. So after disinfecting. your clothes looked worse than before. Therefore, whenever Entlausung was announced ahead of time, I arrived back at camp in my work uniform, leaving the good one in the shop. But whenever our block was ordered for disinfection suddenly during the evening roll call, I had to run to my Jewish friends in the Kleiderkammer Kommando and get from them a temporary set of clothes that could be mutilated in the Entlausung process.

It is appropriate to note here that lice were a big problem in Dora. They were dangerous and unpleasant for the Häftlinge but also very unpleasant for the SS authorities. They were not prepared for how to cope with it. In other concentration camps, they did not pay much attention to it; in fact, lice helped them kill people. Here, however, they had to preserve their work force. Moreover, we were working together with civilians, and those insects could be easily transferred to them. Considerable efforts were undertaken to control this plague. To my recollection, twice we even received vaccine shots against typhoid. However, the most effective method to fight lice was to keep clean. To keep clean, a person has to be fed enough and have enough sleep, time, water, and soap. So by midsummer of 1944, several blocks including ours were virtually cleared of lice. In my opinion, this was only possible because the high authorities of Nazi Germany decided to recognize us as *Schwerarbeiter* (hard working people), who deserved more than two thousand calories of nutrition per day.

In practical terms, this more than doubled our food rations. One can speculate that this amazing decision was connected with the Nazi losses on all fronts and, in particular, with the Allied invasion of Normandy. V-2 rockets were desperately needed. The Savatzki Kommando, under pressure, said that he couldn't produce because 85 percent of his labor force was hungry and tired, so for the sake of victory, they decided to feed and treat us better.

With adequate food, shorter roll calls, and improved sanitary and health care, our life became more bearable. We had enough time to wash ourselves thoroughly and even wash our underwear when we considered it necessary. Many hours were spent looking for lice in our clothes and killing them with our fingernails. Within a week or two of this prosperity, there were no Muselmanen, and all the Häftlinge started to look like human beings. One could say it was no longer a concentration camp; it resembled, rather, a military labor organization because efficient work became the only purpose of our existence. However, the work was demanded and enforced mercilessly.

This was particularly true in the tunnels of the Savatzki Kommando. In each Halle, there were now more civilian supervisors and one or two SS men always present. Nobody could take it easy. For sluggishness in work, the Häftlinge were sentenced to be flogged, and for doing something that could be considered sabotage, they were hung. Those executions were performed publicly during the roll call of the entire camp to scare everybody. This, of course, reminded us that we were still inmates dependent on the whim and mercy of our SS overlords. Except for this terror, things were getting better and better. As mentioned before, we received cigarettes or tobacco and were even paid for the work! Yes! We received the "Lagermarks" (camp money) but not much and in irregular amounts. I do not remember how this was calculated. Anyway, this money could be spent in the canteen. The canteen was opened in one of the new barracks erected across the street from the Arbeitsstatistik office near the Appellplatz. One could buy beer, cigarettes, and cured snails. I'll refrain from describing the quality of these products, but they were there.

Only a part of this barrack was used for the canteen. The bigger portion of it was designated to be a theater or a concert hall. And as unbelievable as it may sound, it was used as such. During the brief periods of relaxation given to us, it became apparent that the inmates of Dora consisted of prominent persons from the populations of lands conquered by the Nazis. Once permitted, this cultural center sprang to life in no time. Several performing arts groups developed, and their shows were excellent. They were compelled to perform in German except for songs and operas, which could be sung in other languages. The best of all was a chamber orchestra composed of twelve to fifteen musicians of different nationalities. Their performances were superior to anything that you could see and hear there. The brass band, playing daily at the gate, was, in its majority, Polish. Occasionally, they also gave concerts in the canteen barracks, but their music was not as sophisticated as that of the chamber orchestra. It was not unusual that SS officers attended the concerts on Sundays with their wives and friends. The first two rows of chairs were always reserved for them. The interior of the rooms in this canteen and theater barracks were beautifully decorated. Each panel of the wall was covered with decorative oil paintings. There were several painters in Dora, mostly French, who created their masterpieces on those walls. All this social and cultural activity remained in sharp contrast with the unpredictability and horrors of our daily life.

This short period of prosperity caused another natural problem: sex. Now when I think of it, I wonder if some SS joker ordered sex-stimulating ingredients to be added to our food. Because in those two summer months of 1944, our sex drives were so intense that one could hardly fight it. And that was true as far as everybody was concerned. At least on our block, people were getting totally disturbed by this urgency. They could not sleep, nor could they walk or behave normally. Masturbation became a common practice, and yet homosexual approaches were few.

Our Blockältester was a homosexual, and he had his "lover"—a pretty-ish Jewish teenager. He was one of the Stubendienst. But they were sleeping together long before this contagious sexual madness popped up. It was, of course, dangerous to be attracted to homosexuals. An approach from a fellow prisoner was not the problem. However, should a Blockältester, Kapo, or Lagerschutz choose you, there was no escape. They could do anything with you—cut your food, transfer you to a bad Kommando, beat you up, or even kill you. The SS authorities were hypocritical in this respect. In the camps, they tolerated it whereas Nazi law considered homosexuality a perversion and dangerous to a healthy society.

The SS also played games with the sexuality of the inmates. At times, when we were sexually aroused, they staged "medical examinations," during which a commission of several SS men and women reviewed our genitals.

They also ran a brothel in the concentration camp using women inmates. After the canteen, this was the second place where one could spend money. Soviets and Jews were prohibited from participation, and for the ordinary Häftling, it was out of reach anyway. One reason was most of them did not have money. The second reason was that in the time available for this pleasure, there were so many candidates that it was almost hopeless to wait in line in particular since the privilege of priority was reserved for all members of the camp administrative staff, according to the hierarchy of their functions.

For a decisive majority of us, the presence of these women in the camp was a serious moral hardship. In fact, all forms of sexual harassment were a terrible depravation of human dignity. It sparked many philosophical discussions among prisoners. There were some who concluded that there was no God! Or if there was, then certainly he was not a loving and just God. "Look," they would say, "innocent people are victims of brutality, persecution on one hand and sexual abuse on the other. They are suffering and dying, unable to prevent it. In the meantime, the tyrants, perverts, assassins, and hangmen are enjoying their kind of life." I did not share this approach. I did not understand God, that's for sure, but I always believed that He is everywhere, that He knows what He is doing and, that in the end justice will prevail. I was praying daily for strength and wisdom to survive or that He would take me to His kingdom.

The season of plenty was short-lived in Dora. In August, the food supply started to decrease. Our SS overlords became harsher again. In particular, their anger concentrated on the Poles. Apparently, the uprising in Warsaw caused it. In the camp proper, many Häftlinge of Polish nationality lost their lucrative functions including the *Lager Dolmetscher*, Ted Pacer. In the Kommandos, more attention was paid to the behavior of the Poles. That resulted in more beatings, kicks, and floggings falling upon them. I was cautious not to give them any opportunity to punish me.

One day, our SS Obersturmführer (the lieutenant in charge of the Außen Kommando) showed up at Niemeier's for a routine inspection. After looking around the plant, he entered Mr. Niemeier's office. A while later, he opened the door, called me in, and said, "You know that conversations between civilians and Häftlinge are prohibited. However, Mr. Niemeier has some questions to ask, which you can answer in my presence." So I was asked if I knew the town of Mława. My answer was that I had never been there but knew where it was. Then he asked "If I knew somebody from this town or its vicinity?" I said no, but I might try to find someone. So, Niemeier said, that he would appreciate any help to find where his son might be. He told me that his son was lost in September 1939, when he was fighting against Polish troops in the region of Mława. He was not recorded as wounded or dead, but perhaps he was injured and maybe found by local people. Then I said that I would ask the people from that region; however, it would be more efficient to ask the Polish welfare organization RGO, which took over most of the agencies of the Polish Red Cross. He appreciated this idea but said, "I doubt that a Polish organization would be willing to help me, especially now that they were cooperating with the Russians." I expressed my surprise and asked, "What makes you think that they are cooperating with the Russians?" He said, "Don't you know that the Poles started an uprising just at the time our troops were fighting the Red Army?" I said that we did not have any radio or press in the camp and that the rumors were not trustworthy, so this was news to me. However, I continued, saying that if that uprising was ordered by the Polish Home Army (AK), operated by the Polish government in exile, then the idea was to liberate part of Poland before it was overrun by the Soviets. This started a conversation in which even *Herr* Obersturmführer participated. I believe that during this conversation, the two Germans understood my Polish reasoning; however, they did not agree with it. Nevertheless, their attitude toward me improved considerably thereafter.

Nothing improved, however, for Hitler's Third Reich. On all fronts, they were in retreat, and Germany proper was under constant air attack. The bombing of German cities was conducted by the British Royal Air Force during the nights whereas Americans did this job during the daytime. For the time being, nobody bombed Dora or Nordhausen. But alarms would go off anytime a raid came close. In the spring of 1944, during daytime hours in Nordhausen, these alarms were sporadic; in the summer, they rang once a week, and in the autumn once every couple of days. At times, Americans flew over Nordhausen in formations consisting of a dozen or two dozen bombers, but sometimes many hundreds of them would go over our heads somewhere further east. Every air raid alarm meant for the workers a pause in their labor. In particular, for us, the Häftlinge, this was a moment of satisfaction that somebody was oppressing our oppressors and also a sign of hope that the end of the oppression was nearing.

There was a rigid rule that during each air raid alarm, everybody had to go to the air raid shelter. There were two such shelters in the Niemeier Vulcanization Werke: one of reinforced concrete under the workshop and the second, a conventional basement under the warehouse. The first one was for the Germans only while the second for foreign workers, but there was nothing for the third-class people—the Häftlinge. When the alarms sounded, we were told to go to the foreigner's shelter. However, soon an order from SS HQ prohibited that and we had to build a third shelter for ourselves. It was a trench dug in the empty space behind the warehouse building. This trench was four to five feet deep and in the shape of a flat letter *W*. Now the segregation was complete, so the Germans could reach their solid bunker in one minute, the foreigners their basement in two minutes, and the inmates their trench in three minutes. Usually, it took us much longer unless rushed by some excited sentries, and often, by the time we reached the trench, the alarm was over.

In a Lager Kommando

By the end of September, we noticed that the supply of raw material—in particular the synthetic rubber used for the tires—was running short. Soon we could not perform our work, and in the early days of October, Niemeier sub-Kommando was dissolved. Even though this was expected, it was a shocking experience in particular because the order came so suddenly and without any warning. One Monday morning, during the roll call preceding the march-out of all the work Kommandos, we heard the loudspeaker announcing, "All Häftlinge of Niemeier Kommando, report to the Lager Kommando!" The Lager Kommando was nothing else but the enlarged and reorganized former Transport Kolonne. It was used now to perform all kinds of odd jobs and to keep all the temporarily unemployed Häftlinge busy. There were more than two hundred of us in this Kommando.

Every morning, after all other Kommandos marched off, the Kapo of the Lager Kommando, assisted by a fellow from the Arbeitsstatistik, assigned his men to different jobs. They had a list of what was to be done and what was urgent. Beginning at the right end of our formation, they detached a group of, say, twenty to unload the railroad cars, ten to clean the SS barracks, five to clean the Revier (hospital facility), and so on. If the work was of a permanent nature, they had a foreman for it, but if it was one or two days of work, they made one of the Häftlinge assigned to the group responsible for it.

On the first day, I was sent with a group of six to move office furniture from one barracks to another, and the second day to dig a trench. By the third morning, I knew already how the system worked, and I realized that the urgent jobs were the toughest ones. So I kept myself on the left end of Lager Kommando formation, where one could be assigned to a less important job. Sure enough, I found myself in a group of about fifteen Häftlinge calling themselves the *Gärtnerei Abteilung*, a landscaping detachment. There were a few French, Jewish, and Russians, but most were Gypsies. One of the Gypsies was considered the leader, and he led us first to a shack where each of us got a tool: a shovel, a spade, a pickax, a rake, a hoe, etc. Then he took us to the place and instructed us on what we should do there. Very soon I realized that neither our leader nor anybody else knew what needed to be done to beautify our camp, the area of which, between the roads and barracks, resembled the surface of the moon. All we did was a simple grading of the rough areas.

When we went to work on the second day in the same group, I asked my Gypsy leader, what would be planted in the ground we were working on. He said that it was not my business; besides, the SS *Scharführer* (so and so) would tell us what to plant here. I said that he, as a Gärtnerei Vorarbeiter, should ask this question ahead of time because the ground needed to be worked differently depending on what was to be planted. My comment piqued his interest, and he asked me with visible curiosity, "How do you know?" When I told him that my father had a big garden and that I myself was a forester, he became very friendly and promised to ask the Scharführer ASAP. The Scharführer's answer was very direct: "You are the gardener. You tell me what you'll plant here!" From then on, I became the professional adviser to the Gypsy "Vorarbeiter."

I showed him where we should plant trees, where to plant grass, and where to prepare soil for flower beds. In only two days, we completed the groundwork of an area between the road and two barracks. Our Gypsy showed it to the Scharführer, explaining what would be planted and where, and the Scharführer said, "*Gut! Gut! Sehr schoen!*" and tapped our foreman on the shoulder. This improved my position considerably. After I offered some tobacco to my Gypsy boss, he became my dedicated friend. Moreover, he considered me to be the boss. He asked me to do nothing but design and stake out the new garden. He grabbed a shovel or rake and started working himself, asking me if he was doing it right.

One day, we ran into big trouble. We were landscaping about half an acre of land behind the kitchen building, enclosed by three roads. In the center of this triangle, I had designed a flower bed in the shape of a star. This shape was clearly visible as a passing SS *Untersturmführer* noticed. He called the foreman. My friend reported to him. The SS man pointed to our work, asking sharply, "*Was ist das?*"

The Gypsy answered, "A flower bed."

"But what is the shape of it?"

"I don't know. He is the layout man," the Gypsy said, pointing to me.

Now I had to answer the SS man's questions, and I said, "A star."

Hearing this, Herr Untersturmführer exploded, saying, "*Warum?* No stars here! *Verboten! Verboten!*"

And I asked, "*Warum?*"

He shouted, "Stars are Soviet, American, not in Deutschland! *Verboten!*"

I attempted to save my design and said, "But sir, this is an eight-pointed star, not five-pointed as theirs."

He was stunned for a second then hit me over the head with the riding whip he had in his hand and shouted, "No stars! *Verstehst du, Idiot!*"

Of course, we had change our star into a rosette by rounding its points. After this incident, my Gypsy friend became very nervous and excited. Later, in a hiding place, when we were smoking our cigarettes, he told me, "Never ever aggravate an SS man." We needed to make them happy because when they were satisfied with our work, as the foreman, he might get a better job. I asked him what he would like to do. And he said, "I am dreaming about being assigned to work in the kitchen."

Two days later, almost the entire Lager Kommando was sent to unload potatoes arriving in railroad boxcars. The first day of this work was very chaotic. With so many workers, the job became very disorganized, with everybody on top of one another. The next day, we were sent in a limited number of forty to fifty men. Our duty was to remove potatoes from the boxcars and deliver them to the long mound where they would be pitted for the winter. Men with potato forks with many prongs close to one another, each with a little knob on the tips, would push the potatoes out of the car and into wheelbarrows. Other Häftlinge then pushed these barrows along a long stretch of single boards laid on the overwhelming mud. They dumped these potatoes onto the staked-out mounds where a few guys with the forks were culling the potatoes and forming mounds to the desired height and shape. Back at the boxcars, at least one-third of the potatoes were missing the wheelbarrows. Those were picked up by another fork man and loaded into the upturned jackets of the Häftlinge who carried them to the mounds—just the same way we moved the dirt in Birkenau.

Since only one row of boards was laid along the track, one could not efficiently unload more than three cars simultaneously. The SS men were rushing the work mercilessly. At each car, there was one of them with a whip, one at the mound, and one along the delivery route. The Häftlinge were bewildered, clumsy, and weak. Our food rations in those days were back to eight hundred calories per twenty-four hours. In this particular turmoil, the French prisoners were at a total loss. They had just arrived from a camp somewhere in France where there was already no work and no food. They now constituted 60 percent of our Lager Kommando. And here, at the potato unloading site, SS men were shouting orders in German, whipping or kicking everyone who immediately did not fulfill these orders.

The French guys were running around in despair, losing their shoes, their canteens, or bowls, which had been attached with string to their belts, and falling down in the mud. Some of the Poles, Russians, and Gypsies were also in the same predicament; however, at least we understood what was going on and what the SS men wanted us to do.

I felt pity for our French comrades, and as much as I could, I tried to explain to them what the SS men wanted. They became effective after they finally understood. In no time, this was noticed by one of the SS men. He approached me and asked, "Hey! *Du! Polski!* What did you say to these French Muselmanen that they started working?"

I said, "I just told them in French what you are ordering!"

"Ah! So! *Gut!* From now on, you'll be the *Vorarbeiter* of this group."

All of a sudden, I was promoted. This was officially confirmed the next morning by the Kapo of the Lager Kommando. I even got a black armband with white lettering saying Vorarbeiter. I led my detachment of thirty-five Frenchmen and fifteen others through the camp gate to our potato battlefield. After the evening conversation with my now "subordinates," we agreed that to save our skin and preserve our potatoes, we had to do our work in an efficient and organized manner. Most of them understood and were cooperating. I explained to all members of my detachment the different functions of our assignment. I believe that everyone understood what he was supposed to do if assigned to one of these functions. Then, during the work, I rotated working men more or less every hour; otherwise, they become exhausted from doing the same work the whole day without any interruption. To everybody's satisfaction, our work was rolling smoothly without hitting and kicking.

Occasionally, shouts were necessary—in particular when someone was keeping others from proceeding, exposing them to SS abuses. During the second day of our organized work, only one SS man remained at the unloaded cars. By the third day, all the cars were unloaded, and my "*Kartoffel* Kommando" went to cover up the mounds with straw and dirt. This was a much easier and less exhausting job, especially since there was no push by the SS to do it in a hurry. Again, my men were instructed on what to do and performed well. In fact, we could have covered up all those potatoes in a few short days. However, there was no reason to hurry. The weather was warm and pleasant, and there was no reason to worry that the potatoes would freeze. So I let my fellows work in two shifts: one working, one resting. This, of course, was against the camp rules whereby every Häftling must be working the whole prescribed time. Therefore, I had to pay particular attention that no SS man caught my men resting, and for a while, it was working well. When I noticed an SS man approaching, I started to shout, and all fifty guys were busy removing rotten potatoes, hauling straw, and digging dirt.

On the second afternoon, I spotted an SS guard with a dog walking our way. As usual, I alerted my Kommando, and the whole crowd of Häftlinge got to work efficiently. The SS man passed by and was already at the end of our mound where the straw was stored in a pile when his dog became restless and started to penetrate the straw with his nose. Alas! Two Russians were sleeping there. The SS man became furious and, with sadistic hatred, started to punish them. He clubbed them with the butt of his rifle, with his fists in the face, and kicked them in any spot possible. While he was mistreating one of the poor fellows, his dog took care of the second one. When they finished their devilish work, my two sleeping Häflinge were also finished. They could not get up; they could not move. Now the still very agitated and visibly tired guard turned to me, hit me in the face, tore off my armband, and ordered me to walk in front of him toward the ramp where the trucks were dumping more potatoes.

At this location, there were many prisoners from different Kommandos working under the supervision of an SS man who was in charge of this potato-unloading operation. He decided that for the reckless performance of my duties as a Vorarbeiter, I be assigned to the Strafe Kommando, or the "penalty division," which was right there. These were two large wooden boxes with shafts projecting from the front and the rear. Those were the handles for two men to carry that box, which, when filled with potatoes, would weigh at least 220 pounds. Prisoners sentenced to be penalized were forced to carry it. When I arrived on the scene, there was, unfortunately, another such punished prisoner already there. He had stolen something from his Blockältester. I was ordered to pick up the box in the front, and the thief in the rear. And then came, "*Los!*" Let's go! We went through the muddy field, about three hundred feet, to the end of another storage mound. Then running back to pick up the second box, filled in the meantime with potatoes. This went on and on. I could not dare fall down because if I did, my legs would be crushed by the heavy box. The guy in the rear fell down several times, but the whips and kicks forced him to move again. Fortunately, after a fifth or sixth box, it became dark, and the work Kommandos had to go back to the camp for "accounting" purposes. I had to walk together with the detachment of the Lager Kommando no more as a *Vorarbeiter* but as one punished for those two sleeping in the straw. I was totally exhausted, and every part of my body was in pain. I knew that a few more hours of this penalty work would finish me off. Therefore, the next morning, I decided to take the most dangerous step: hide and not report to work. After the morning roll call, instead of joining the Lager Kommando, I disappeared in the darkness of the misty pre-dawn. After all the Kommandos left the camp, I sneaked into block 104, where my friend Tadek (his last name, I cannot recall) was the *Blockschreiber*. He hid me in a closet and went to the Arbeitsstatistik to see his friends working there in an attempt to solve my problem in a more formal manner.

Fortunately, that was possible because the SS man who con-demned me to the penalty work acted in haste and did not take down my number. Within the Lager Kommando, my French friends (subordinates for four days) convinced the Kapo that I was sick. All of them, one louder than the other, were screaming, "*Oh! Monsieur le Vorarbeiter! Malade! Beaucoup malade!*" So after Tadek spoke to his friends in the Arbeitsstatistik, they recorded me as sick in the hos-pital (Revier). Of course, the *Revierschreiber* had to put my number on their list. It was terribly embarrassing and troubling to me that so many people had to risk so much, possibly even their lives, to help me. But I was still in a very complicated predicament. Once recorded in the hospital, I should be there and not in my block—number 25. The evening roll call would certainly reflect this.

So for the head count to be correct, I went to the hospital and lay down along the wall of one of the barracks and pretended to be a rejected, dying Muselman. But I did not want to be actually admitted to that sickening facility. So Tadek took the risk again and managed to let me sleep in his block. The next day, since the higher authorities did not ask where I was, the Polish guys in the Arbeitsstatistik sent me to the Kapo of the kitchen who had requested two potatoes peelers. That evening, I reported back to my block, and the next morning to the Kommando whose only duty was to peel the potatoes. It was considered an exclusive Kommando. Only privileged prisoners could be admitted there. After all, it was within the cooking facility, and nobody working there was ever hungry.

All Häftlinge working in the kitchen as well as in the so-called supply column (Versorgung Kolonne) slept in the same block (number 102, as far as I remember), so I had to move there. Kitchen workers consisted, of course, of cooks, cook helpers, vegetable handlers, dishwashers, etc., but most numerous were the peelers of potatoes. There were maybe twenty-five of them. The majority were Polish intellectuals. So far so good; however, the work itself was no fun whatsoever. Twelve hours per day, we had to sit on a low bench in a damp, stinky room, electric lights barely penetrating the steaming air. Between the legs of each peeler, there was a basket for the peels and a container for the peeled potatoes. In between each two peelers was a container with potatoes. One had to peel clean and fast without wasting too much of the precious substance of the potato. Your basket and container were numbered, and the cook helpers receiving it were carefully controlling the quantity and quality of your work. If you did not meet expectations, you were fired—back to being hungry in Lager Kommando. I wonder how long they would have tolerated me there if not for the power of the tobacco, of which some quantity I succeeded to preserve.

As I mentioned before, the people from the supply column lived in the same barracks. It was a very unusual Kommando handling all the food for the camp that housed at that time about thirty-thousand prisoners. They operated several huge trucks that drove to different, sometimes distant, locations where the food was available.

The most unusual part of this was their unprecedented freedom. The prisoners performed their duties alone without any supervision and virtually without guards. Their Kapo, an Austrian political prisoner, was authorized to sign receipts and payment vouchers. Drivers of the trucks were prisoners, and almost all of them wore civilian clothes. However, these were painted with red stripes. They were, of course, the wealthiest of all Häftlinge.

I write about them to illustrate that it was not easy for a prisoner to escape Nazi Germany not because of all the fences, guards, and dogs but the efficiency of the security system and the cooperation of the entire population. For instance, it would be no problem for me, a prisoner, to leave Niemeier's plant unnoticed. But the alarm would be sounded in an hour or two at best. And where would I go after leaving the plant? I didn't know anyone in the center of Germany. The Kapo of the supply column was in a much better position: he had no language problem, he had acquaintances, and he had money, cars, and much, much more time than anybody; and yet three months after he ran, they brought him back. This occurred during the one week I lived in block number 102 and worked in the kitchen.

And so now I ran into my Gypsy friend in the Lager Kommando. He was still there. When he heard that I was working in the kitchen, his astonishment, envy, and sorrow were indescribable. And yet my career as a potato peeler ended as abruptly as it began.

Kommando Niemeier was reestablished again. By the end of October, we were vulcanizing tires in an accelerated tempo, trying to catch up with the backlog, which developed in the previous four weeks. There were some differences, however. The raw rubber, which was brought in from who knows where, was of lesser quality and demanded more work and attention. It was obvious that the repaired tires would not last long. The Belgian fellow was no longer with us, and the SS ran out of trucks for the transportation of prisoners to many workshops. Somehow, they managed to drive us in the mornings using private, rundown trucks powered by wood gas. In the evenings, however, we had to walk those five or six kilometers from the plant to the camp. This was disliked by the SS guardsmen and extremely harsh for those of us who had bad shoes.

I personally enjoyed these walks. The road through the beautiful hilly countryside, covered in colorful foliage, in particular on a bright day was a pleasant break from the shop and the camp. But in the camp, things were worsening. In particular, food rations were shrinking, and SS roughness was growing. Food was getting short for everybody. Lunch sandwiches for the SS guardsmen became very small indeed. Our German work masters visibly lost weight and spirit. French and Byelorussian workers were outright hungry. Thus, one could get lots of tobacco for a loaf of bread. But it was also difficult to find a loaf of bread, even for those in the Versorgung Kolonne.

The new Zugangs who were arriving almost daily made the problem even more difficult. Many of these new prisoners were civilians from Warsaw. Under international pressure, Germans recognized the Polish Home Army (AK) fighting in the Warsaw uprising as a regular army and, according to the Geneva Convention, locked them up in POW camps. However, the civilian population was forced out of the city before its methodical destruction to temporary camps in the suburbs then segregated, and most of the capable men were sent to concentration camps. With their arrival, I had the opportunity to meet many fine people. It was as if the last college-educated people of prewar Poland were shipped out of the country. University professors, PhD holders, lawyers, physicians, engineers—hundreds of them, mistreated, hungry, and not protected from the cold, were deteriorating in the overcrowded camp Dora. I developed friendly relationships with two of the newcomers. Mr. Wroblewski, who had a PhD in physics and whose father was the codiscoverer of oxygen, and Mr. Lipinski, a mechanical engineer and also an astronomer. Somehow, they were lodged in my block, and we stood for hours on the Appellplatz during, again, longer evening roll calls. Grateful for our endless talks about uprisings, politics, astronomy, physics, and our future, I provided them with cement bags that were used as vests under their jackets as excellent protection against the penetrating frigid wind. I taught them how to keep themselves warm and how to prevent frostbite, and whenever I succeeded in securing extra bread, I shared it with them.

Coinciding with the Germans' misfortunes on the battlefields and with the shortages of supplies, the terror of the SS grew in our camp. They were always merciless in regard to those prisoners who attempted to run, sabotage the work, or get involved in some kind of political activity or conspiracy. However, in the last quarter of 1944, for some reason, the number of such "criminal incidents" increased dramatically. I think that it was rather the number of public executions that increased. One of those we were forced to witness was the hanging of four prisoners. One of them was that fugitive Kapo of the supply column. Another one was apparently dumping sand into some V-2 equipment. And the other two were accused of conspiracy against the SS rulers of the camp.

This last accusation we heard for the first time, yet months before, I heard rumors that some kind of underground organization was operating inside Camp Dora. I have no doubt that somebody had a radio receiver in the camp because the news of the progress of the war was spreading among prisoners before it could be confirmed by those having access to German newspapers. And as far as the "organization" is concerned, I do not know personally about it. I do suspect that it could have been a communist initiative and that these guys knew well that I was not one of them.

Our miserable life was shocked for one week in December when we were ordered to remain in the camp and not to go to Niemeier's. Nobody knew why, and so it took us by surprise. It became a very hungry week. Camp rations, without any supplement, turned out to be insufficient this time. I remember digging turnip peels out of the mud near the SS kitchen then cooking it in my mess can over the illegal campfire. The taste of this so-called soup was horrible, but a hungry person will eat everything. As it turned out, this concentration camp diet ruined my stomach for the rest of my life.

Shortly before Christmas, we started traveling to Nordhausen again. This somewhat improved our situation, but we felt that it wouldn't last for very long. Nevertheless, the Christmas of 1944 in Dora was much better than the year before. For one, in some unusual humanitarian (or hypocritical) gesture, the SS commander of the camp, *Sturmbannführer* Otto Forschner, ordered that Christmas carols would be played on Christmas Eve. First, the camp band played live, then they let us listen to records on the loudspeaker system. Of course, most of the carols were German, but there were a few French and even two Polish ones. That could have been somehow inspiring if not for the cold, in which we had to stand for one extra hour while listening to the music. In the barracks, however, we did everything that we could to celebrate this Holy Night as festively as possible.

Each national group assembled at their own tables. The Poles and Czechs managed to have a little Christmas tree decorated with some toys made of wood and acorns and foil saved from the parcels we received. We managed to save some food for this particular occasion. One of our fellow prisoners—I think a priest, very skinny and weak—said the prayer, which was, in stark contrast to his appearance, strong in faith and love. We ate tiny pieces of bread, wished one another a Merry Christmas, sang our traditional carols, and smoked cigarettes made with my tobacco wrapped in the paper from a cement bag. Despite the hunger and sickness of many comrades, our mood was glorious and full of hope that this was the last Christmas in captivity.

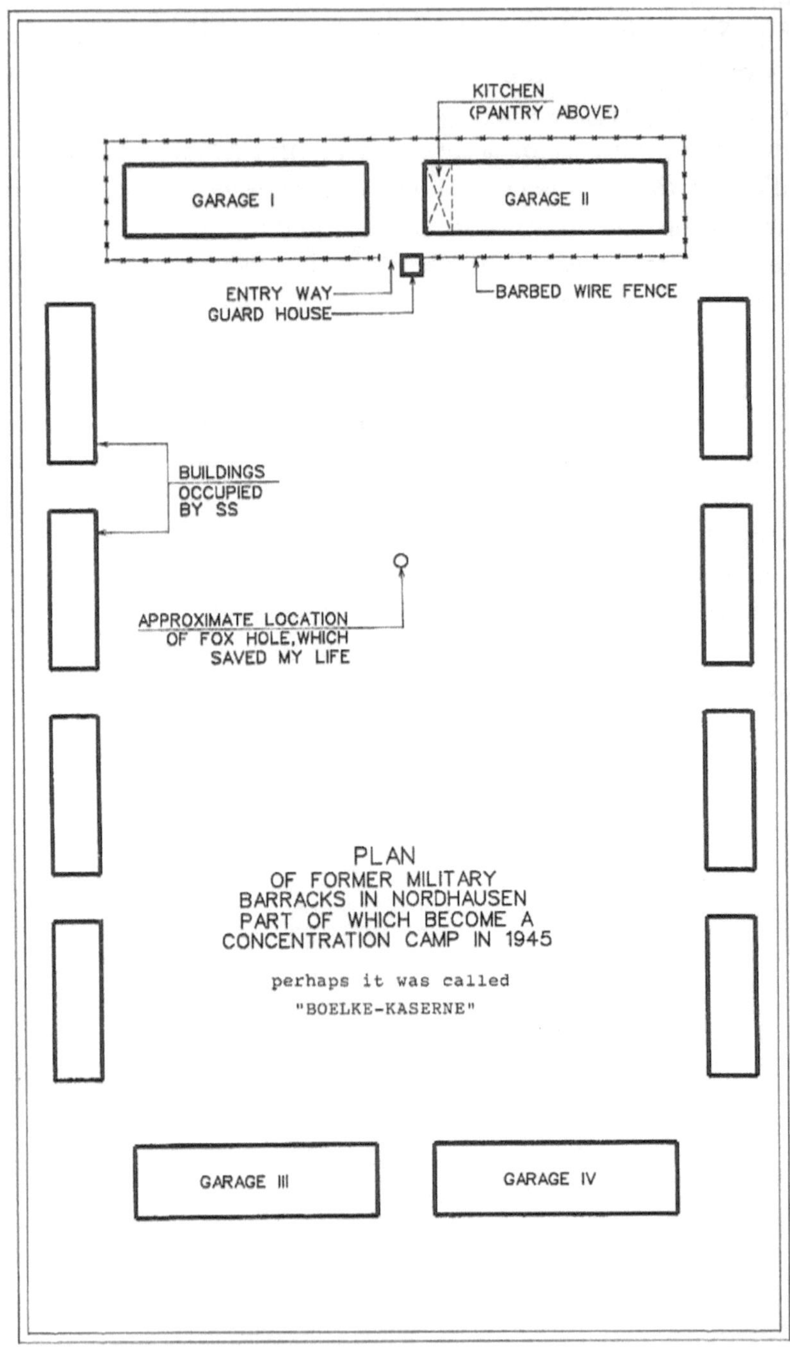

KITCHEN
(PANTRY ABOVE)
GARAGE I
GARAGE II
ENTRY WAY
GUARD HOUSE
BARBED WIRE FENCE
BUILDINGS
OCCUPIED
BY SS
APPROXIMATE LOCATION
OF FOX HOLE, WHICH
SAVED MY LIFE
PLAN
OF FORMER MILITARY
BARRACKS IN NORDHAUSEN
PART OF WHICH BECOME A
CONCENTRATION CAMP IN 1945
perhaps it was called
"BOELKE-KASERNE"
GARAGE III
GARAGE IV

CHAPTER 9

Nordhausen, Boelcke-Kaserne

On January 10, 1945, we did not return to Dora from our vulcanization shop. Instead we walked the opposite way—across the town of Nordhausen to a new camp. To solve the problems of transportation and that of overcrowding in Camp Dora, SS authorities surrounded with a barbed wire fence a couple of two-story-high garages. These were part of the military barracks located in the industrial area of the town, not far from the railway depot.

Originally parked on the ground level of these buildings were heavy military equipment, I think probably tanks. The second floor, a huge attic, could have been used as the storage of materials. Unfenced, these two garages were part of the military barracks of a layout typical in Germany. Two identical garages were also on the opposite end of a big yard approximately 250 feet wide and 500 feet long. On each side of this yard, there were four barracks for soldiers. Each had two or three dormitory floors and a basement. All these buildings were of masonry construction. One or two of these dormitory buildings were occupied by SS troops, and the rest by civilian foreign workers. The only entrance to our enclosure was from the yard. The fence did not have any watchtowers, so SS guards patrolled the perimeter.

The entire Außen Kommando—that is, all work detachments working in Nordhausen—now counting about five hundred men, were transferred to this new camp in the city and housed in one half of the second floor of one of the garages. This was a huge space with the rough underside of the sloping roof as its ceiling. The space was filled with wooden beds identical to those in the barracks of Dora except that they were four levels high in the center of the room then lower and lower and finally, single beds near the eave of the roof. Unfortunately, there was only one staircase to this space, which was located near the center of the garage. An identical set of stairs led to the attic space over the second half of the garage. The toilet facilities were installed between these two sets of stairs.

On the first floor, the last bay of one of the garages was walled off by a masonry wall, and in this twenty-foot-wide space was the kitchen with food storage upstairs. There was not much space between the garage buildings and the surrounding fence, so it was the only camp without an Appellplatz. However, there was enough room for five rows of Häftlinge for a roll call. This ritual was meticulously performed in the mornings and evenings. Fortunately, it took much less time here. Now we walked to our shop both ways, which took forty minutes each way. We walked through the city, bypassing the center of town.

There was ample work at Niemeier's but no food. That was because our rations became ridiculously small and irregular. There was no way to supplement it whatsoever. We were losing weight to the point that there was nothing more to lose. One of the four German masters in our shop (I think his first name was Paul) was openly appalled by our condition. In a truly humanitarian gesture, he took it upon himself every morning to bring a couple of gallon buckets of soup cooked by his wife. They did not have much to eat themselves, yet they found a few potatoes, vegetables, or grit to provide some nourishment for us. I prayed for them daily, but Nicolai maintained the opinion that Paul was certainly a communist.

Paul's initiative combined with our miserable condition and poor performance as workers prompted the Niemeier company to start giving us a bowl of soup daily. This, reluctantly, was approved by the SS authorities, provided that soup was also available for their sentries guarding us.

So much for the body. There was much more for our spirit. Signs of Hitler's crumbling might were everywhere—no supplies, no transportation, more wounded and exhausted soldiers, and many civilian fugitives in the streets. But the frequency and size of the air raids were most convincing. Now Americans were flying over Nordhausen every day, and sometimes the number of airplanes was uncountable. Squadron after squadron, from left to right across the sky, were planes moving in waves over our heads, wave after wave, with the monotonous deep roar of their engines. Of course, each such flight was preceded by a *Fliegeralarm*. The sirens sang their protracted "melody," announcing approaching danger. Everybody would stop working and proceed to his shelter. We, the prisoners, had the longest way to go, but we were never in a hurry. Accustomed to danger and death, we moved slowly. Our SS guards, usually very excited by the alarm, rushed us to speed up. In most instances, when we reached our trench, the sirens sounded the all clear. The several short interconnected whistles would sound as if rejoicing that the danger was over. So we started our promenade back to the shop. Usually, it took fifteen to twenty minutes of our work time. But sometimes, when a large armada moved across the sky, we would sit on the bank of the shelter trench, attempting to count the airplanes. The SS men, trying to cover up their frustration, ordered us to hide in the trench without much success, however.

In the meantime, the camp in the garages was filled to capacity. In the last days of February, several evacuation transports arrived. The biggest one, able to carry about two thousand men, was from Gross-Rosen, a camp located in Northwestern Silesia (the territory that, before September 1, 1939, was within the German Reich). It was proof that the eastern front was now moving westward very fast. The evacuated prisoners were in terrible condition. Very few of them resembled normal people. About 75 percent were to be classified as Muselmanen, and 24 percent were already so sick that they could not move on their own. The life in Gross-Rosen was terrible to begin with, then the ordeal of the transport, which took many days and, above all, caused more hunger, devastated these people. Those who were still walking on their own legs were accommodated in the second garage, but the sick and dying were packed solid on the first floor of the first garage, right below our quarters. The sight of this so-called sick ward was absolutely horrible. Suffering and dying skeletons lay next to one another on the entire huge concrete floor of this garage. There were no alleys between these bodies for access. Few so-called medics were assigned to this "Revier." However, their only function was to carry out cadavers and pile them up at the stairways near the exit doors. Once every two or three days, these skin-covered skeletons were thrown into a truck that took them to Dora's crematorium.

The handling of the corpses by these orderlies was itself a horribly grotesque sight. Even though the corpses were not that heavy, the orderlies themselves were weak and unfit to do anything. They had to step over those still living, carrying a dead body by the legs and hands. Time and again, one of them tripped and fell, pulling with him the corpse together with the second orderly, or dropping the corpse so that it landed on the miserable creatures that were still alive. Perhaps a more practical method would be to pull the corpse by the legs over the bodies of living comrades. On the other hand, in this hall of death full of groans and stench, one could see a figure or two moving from one sick man to another one, talking to them, listening to them, and giving their consolation or absolution. Obviously, these were a few priest prisoners who performed their spiritual duties in any circumstances until the last breath of their own. Among the Zugangs were many evacuees from Auschwitz. Most of them were Poles, but there were also a few Russians, Jews, and Gypsies. They told me that as they were leaving Auschwitz, they could hear the roar of the approaching front. Obviously, the majority of them had numbers higher than mine; however, I did not see any number higher than 202150. Anyway, by the end of March, there were about three thousand prisoners in our camp in Nordhausen, five hundred workers upstairs, five hundred sick downstairs, and two thousand Muselmanen in the remaining parts of the two garages.

By March, everybody in Nordhausen became accustomed to the air raid alarms. Day after day was the same routine: sirens; airplanes appearing in the sky, roaring overhead, and disappearing in the east; and sirens again. I think it was March 31 or April 1. The day was nice and quiet. At noontime, while eating our Niemeier soup, we wondered why the Americans were not flying today. But one or two hours after lunch, the alarm sounded and allowed us to drop our tools. Walking along the warehouse wall toward our trench, we noticed three small airplanes just over our heads. They spread apart and started to circle, releasing smoke streaks. We looked at one another, and without a word, we understood. It was time to run! Somebody shouted, "*Schnell! Sie werden bombardieren!*"

Guided apparently by some instinct, the two civilian Frenchmen jumped out of their shelter under the warehouse and ran with us. When we reached our trench, the planes were already visible, approaching in tight formations lower than usual. We jumped into the trench. On my right were the two wary-looking, cynical Frenchmen, and on my left two heroes of the godless Soviet Union. The others were further away whereas one SS guard took a position at each end of the trench. These guys attempted to remain on top of the bank but only until the first bombs started to hit the ground. The attack was immediately ferocious. The bombs hit the ground simultaneously, causing a terrifying roar. Instantly several railway boxcars just outside Niemeier's property burst into flames. So did shanties on the adjoining properties. Burning pieces of wood and rubber flew, hissing over our heads. The closer explosions rocked the earth. Choking black smoke engulfed us. And into this terrible inferno, more bombs started to fall, exploding closer and closer to our miserable trench.

It was really scary. I started to pray "*Pod Twoją Obrone,*" a Polish prayer asking the Holy Mother of God to protect us. But my concentration was interrupted by the unusual behavior of my neighbors. The Frenchmen were beaming with joy, exclaiming in strident shouts, "*Oh, merde! Ça va bien! Très bien! Très bien. Enfin les des bombes sont finis!*" They almost jumped out of the trench to dance in exaltation. Yet on my left, the Russians pressed their heads into the side of the trench, covered their back with a blanket, and, pounding their chests with their fists, cried, "*Gospodi pomyluy! Gospodi pomyluy!*" (God have mercy!)

And God obviously was pleased with that outburst of belief by the declared atheists and let the Americans move their bombing to other parts of the city. Nevertheless, we could not get out of our shelter because everything around us was on fire. Empty shanties, boxcars full of lumber and clothing, cisterns with liquid fuel, factories, and warehouses including our warehouse, which was loaded with tires and other rubber products, were all in a raging fire.

The bombardment was over, and the planes were gone. But there were no sirens announcing Entwarnung. After a long while, our guards decided that we had to get out. As we did, we immediately realized that we would not be working at Niemeier's anymore. One bomb hit the west wall of the warehouse, opening its entire side. The contents and the roof were in flames. The workshop had been hit by two or maybe three bombs because it was totally in ruins. From the looks of it, we concluded that the shelter *nur für Deutsche* collapsed also. The shelter *für die Auslaender* was holding, but the fire above was making it difficult to escape. The SS guards did not permit us to attempt to look for survivors. Only the French guys ran to look for their Byelorussian boys, who might still be in the basement. We, the Häftlinge, the eight men who worked in this plant for more than a year, had to just march by its ruins, leaving behind the other eight workers—eight maybe not friends but coworkers. These were eight human beings who were more good than bad. In any case, they were deserving of some help. However, the SS rushed us to be in camp before dark.

It was a long and difficult walk. The streets were covered with rubble and, in some places, completely blocked by fallen buildings or huge bomb craters. It was astonishing to see how much destruction had been caused by this raid, which lasted no more than twenty minutes. After more than an hour of walking through this mess, we arrived at our camp. What we found was not looking like the camp anymore. There were just two severely damaged garage buildings. The barbed wire fence was almost gone, including the gate and the guardhouse. The real disaster, however, was in the so-called sick ward. A few bombs hit the ground right next to the building, blowing the wall inside and igniting the straw, which had been delivered there just a few days before. That ended the suffering of all five hundred occupants of the ward. Their bodies were still burning at the time of our arrival, smelling horribly. The second building was also hit, but the extent of damage was less severe. The two thousand Muselmanen living there succeeded in extinguishing the fire. A bomb also hit one of the SS dormitory buildings.

We joined a few other work Kommandos that arrived ahead of us and now stood on the street outside the camp area, surrounded by numerous SS guards. We waited for an hour or more until all the Kommandos returned from their shops. SS officers were running like mad here and there. From the ruins of their guardhouse, they dug out a telephone and reestablished communication. They made and received many calls. A rumor spread among the prisoners that they were looking for transportation to ship us to Dora. This attempt failed.

Late that evening, they ordered us into our dormitory "block." This was no fun either. Our beds were on the floor above the "sick ward," and that floor was cracked and dangerously tilted. It did not collapse because the reinforcing bars were holding the concrete together. Our leaning beds threatened to collapse anytime. And the stench from downstairs! It was a terrible night: hungry, stinking, and chaotic. However, our spirits were high. The end of our ordeal was very close—close but in an unpredictable manner. Ultimately, it was tragic for so many.

There was no reveille whistle in the morning as usual, and we stayed in our beds until it became light outside. Through the few remaining windows, we could see that our SS caretakers had not had an easy night either. After replacing the destroyed fence, they spent the entire night standing around the two garages filled with their "Banditen." Nothing indicated that they were going to give us anything to eat or drink or that they would take some Kommandos to work. We expected that at any minute, they would have us go to Dora, if not by truck then on foot.

At about 10:00 a.m., there was a sudden commotion outside. Many people appeared outside the buildings as well as in the yards between the military barracks and in the streets nearby. The chain of SS men around our buildings sprang to life. The guardsmen were talking in excitement with one another and looking around as if they needed to find something important. Then suddenly airplanes appeared in the western sky. It was then we understood: the alarm system was destroyed by yesterday's bombardment, so people learned about any new danger by telephone or radio. And sure enough, the scout planes started their marking maneuvers.

After yesterday's experience, we immediately became terrified and wanted to run. But that meant getting shot by the SS guardsmen. But no! Look! The SS men were running! Army soldiers were running! Crowds of civilians were running! Let's go! Hurry! Hurry! With unbelievable speed, hundreds of my roommates ran to the stairs and down, jumping over one another. I hated crowds and congestion. I thought it was better to be killed by the bombs than trampled by my comrades. I told this to my bed neighbor Edek, a Polish fellow about twenty years older than I. He agreed and suggested, "Let's take our canteens and blankets!" This we did.

Near our beds, we encountered a totally bewildered young Belgian boy. We calmed him down and told him to follow us. When we got out of our garage, a few Muselmanen were lingering outside the second garage. The majority of them remained inside, physically and mentally unable to run to safety. Between the military barracks, ahead of us, an enormous crowd was running away into the empty garden and the fields beyond. I only saw the backs of the people running in that crowd—civilian men and women, Germans and Auslaender (foreigners), and Army soldiers and SS men, all together with our comrades in their striped uniforms. We were far behind, and it seemed hopeless for us to reach the open field in particular since the enormous air armada was already in full sight. We were in the center of the yard surrounded by the dormitory barracks and the garages. I noticed that there were several foxholes dug in this yard. I called to Edek and the Belgian, "Jump into the nearest hole." So they did, Edek a few steps ahead and the Belgian a few steps to my left as I was looking for a hole a bit farther to the right. But in that moment, I noticed that the bombs started coming down like strings of beads from each plane in the front row. Without hesitating, I jumped into the same hole occupied by Edek. It was tight—in particular when we bent our legs to hide our heads as low as possible. We covered ourselves with our blankets. In that moment, all hell broke loose!

Bombs were hitting everywhere and everything like hailstones, one every sixty feet in each direction. The earth trembled with interlocking roars of explosions, and debris started falling on our blankets. Then came a terrible shock right in front of us, and a mass of earth rose to cover us up. Another shock came close behind us, and a second pile of earth landed on us. The deafening noise of the raid became suddenly dampened. We were buried alive under a heavy pile of dirt!

A dreadful panic overwhelmed me. Edek screamed, "Jesus, Maria, we will suffocate! Let's push it up! Now together! One, two, three! Up!" Alas! The load pressing down on us did not move whatsoever.

We were in a very awkward position. To develop any appreciable leverage, we had to move, but any adjustment of our bodies was extremely difficult. Fortunately, the blankets on our backs formed a vault under which several cubic feet of air remained below us, surrounding our legs. I was able to move my right hand and attempted to force it up through the loose earth above me. My elbow hit a wooden pole that was standing in the corner of our foxhole. I started to work my hand along this pole. The dirt was slowly trickling down my arm as I pushed my hand up. It was working but so, so slow. My arm was in pain and losing strength. Worst, we were running out of air in our grave. I was on the verge of fainting, but with the last effort, I pushed my hand up. And suddenly it went easy. More dirt slithered in, and with it fresh air. Thanks to you, oh Lord! What a relief! I rested for a while then started to enlarge the vent shaft between my arm and that pole. Soon there was enough air that we could breathe easy and regain our strength. Pulling up on the pole, I could inch up my body. This gave some room for Edek to change his cramped position. Now we again made a combined effort to push up our burden, this time with success. Suddenly we emerged at the top of a heap of loose, fresh soil. The relief and happiness that we felt from being outof the grave was so great that another wave of airplanes and bombs would not have scared us a bit.

We sat at the top of our hill, breathing deeply and looking around at the moonlike landscape surrounding us. The buildings that surrounded the huge yard, in the middle of which was our foxhole, were gone or almost gone, some burning, others smoking. So were all the buildings outside of our barracks, as far as our eyes could see. All around us, the earth was churned upside down. There were no lawns, pavements, or gardens.

Everywhere, there were only piles of dirt and bomb craters. From the sloping side of the crater, which was next to the pile upon which we were sitting, protruded the upper part of the body of our Belgian friend. His head and chest were fully exposed and clean of dirt. His young face, as if still alive, was turned up, looking into the sky, from which the bombs came, blowing his soul out of his body.

The bombing now moved on to more distant parts of the town. We decided to go and look at our garage camp. Only reinforced concrete skeletons of both buildings remained. Surprisingly, the gable bay of one of them retained part of the second floor and a few partitions. It was the camp food storage. And the food was still there! Loaves of bread were on racks, and some cartons and cans were spread out along the hanging floor, under which the kitchen equipment was smoldering. The heat melted the margarine upstairs, and it was running down the sloping floor and dripping off the ends of the broken reinforcement bars. Underneath, on a pile of rubble, two or three Muselmanen were scrambling and trying to catch the dripping fat. It was not possible to get up to where the food was. There were no stairs or ladders, and besides, that floor was barely hanging on and could collapse into the fire anytime.

Except for these few Muselmanen, there were no people in sight. Edek and I found ourselves free. What should we do now? We decided that the first thing to do was to get some civilian clothing. Therefore, we went to the buildings that were occupied by the civilian foreign workers. Unfortunately, all these barracks were totally destroyed. It was not possible to find anything in the piles of rubble. The lower half of one of the buildings, where the SS guards used to live, was still standing, so we went there in the hope of finding something useful. And we did—shoes and food! My beneficial shoes, which I got in the parcel, were already falling apart, so the new military footwear was just in time. And in a small pantry in the basement, there were a dozen loaves of bread, some margarine, and marmalade. We ate in a hurry as much as we could. Then we found some canvas handbags, which we filled solid with bread, probably about six pounds. Then we left the destroyed barracks and went toward the open fields.

Eerie were those gardens and semiempty spaces where, at the beginning of the raid, thousands of people ran for their lives. Most didn't run fast enough. Now their torn bodies were mixed thoroughly with the soil upon which they ran. It was a horrible, bloody field. Human body parts were everywhere, most of them partially buried in dirt, partially projecting above it. There were separate legs, hands, heads, and intestines. Entangled in torn clothing were women, men, civilians, and military, all mixed in the bloody mud. We hurried as fast as we could across this butcher's field, paying no attention to pieces of civilian clothing, even in wearable condition, lying here and there.

Finally, we were out into the fields where the bombs did not fall. Here we encountered other survivors of this devastating raid. More and more people fleeing a destroyed burning city appeared on the unpaved, muddy paths leading out into the country. We joined that crowd and kept moving away from the town.

After a few minutes of such dragging, we came upon two women with two children who were begging for help. Nobody paid any attention to their entreaties, so we decided to help them. Apparently, one was the grandmother, and the second the mother of a three- or four-year-old girl and a baby in a carriage. This flimsy vehicle broke under the weight of the goods stuffed in with the baby. The mother seemed to be ill or wounded. She could not do anything. We attempted to pull the baby carriage, but the already twisted wheels did not rotate and cut deep into the mud. We detached the wheels, and both of us together pulled the carriage with its bottom sliding on the dirt and mud. The younger women and the girl walked ahead of us, the grandma behind.

After twenty or thirty minutes, we reached an intersection with a major road. From the ditch along that road, a lone SS man with a gun in his hand emerged suddenly. In just a few leaps, he was next to us, shouting that we should drop the carriage and follow the highway toward the town. Both women started to cry and begged him to let us stay and help them, but the SS man said that Edek and I were dangerous "bandits" and that for the benefit of *Großdeutschland*, we must be locked up. So we left that helpless family, and with the gun pointed at our backs, we followed this fanatic's orders. We came to a shanty where there were some other SS men and a few captured "fugitives." A while later, a few more "fugitives" were brought, but this time by the Volkssturm people. These were old men and teenagers called to arms to defend the *Vaterland*. Many of them still believed in German superiority and could be very dangerous.

We were moving slowly to the southwest, guarded by three SS troopers, whereas several other SS men and Volkssturm people were combing the territory around Nordhausen in search for more scattered Häftlinge. By sunset, they had assembled twenty-four of us. And this was all that remained that walked on their own two feet from the camp of 3,500 souls just twenty-four hours before. Perhaps a few more succeeded in hiding somewhere, but many, however, were disabled and lying within the ruins of the buildings or in the bomb craters. Several months after the war, I heard from UNRRA that after the Americans entered Nordhausen, they found about two hundred ex-prisoners still alive; however, not many of them survived despite considerable efforts on the part of the Allied medical personnel.

When the sun disappeared behind the hills, we, still surrounded by SS guards, started toward Camp Dora. This walk across the countryside took at least two hours. When we arrived at the gate, it was very dark. The local guards did not appreciate our arrival. They did not let us in and ordered us off the main road. No lights were on, neither inside the camp, on the fence, nor in the SS quarters. Yet there was considerable commotion in the camp and at the railway yard. After lots of orders and shouts, the gate opened, and to our surprise, columns of prisoners began walking out of the camp. They were in formation, not looking like work Kommandos but, size wise, corresponding to the dormitory blocks. It dawned on us that this was the evacuation of the camp.

After about ten blocks went out the gate, they finally admitted us inside. There, after our numbers were recorded by the two Arbeitsstatistik officials, the Lagerschutz directed us into one of the empty barracks for the night. We asked for some food, but the camp policemen, who were about to leave, just laughed. However, I asked them to show me to the kitchen. In the kitchen, I met some of the fellows with whom I had worked half a year before. They remembered me and my tobacco. They were also very excited to hear about the destruction of Nordhausen, so they found one kettle of soup and even helped me take it to our barracks, which was nearby. The soup and the long quiet night of sleep helped us regain our strength for the long journey ahead. The evacuation of the camp was proceeding throughout the next day. Barracks after barracks were called out, arranged in formation, for the roll call, checked out by SS officers and the Arbeitsstatistik officials. Then we marched in normal *"zu fünf"* formation to the gate. Many of the Blockältester, Lagerschutz, and other camp officials stayed behind. Were they also being evacuated? I do not know. Finally, they called out our block, and we ran hurriedly through the gate and along a long train of boxcars and piled into the last half-empty one. There were all together—about fifty prisoners—in this the last car of the train.

Before the train moved, we got food for the trip: one loaf of bread each and a small tin of marmalade for two. This was a luxury since many evacuation trains left without any food, not to speak of the evacuation convoys on foot, which, as a general rule, ended in total disaster. Two SS guardsmen took their positions—one in front and one in the rear of the car. They sat on either side of the car, facing the living cargo inside. In the late afternoon of April 3, 1945, our train started rolling. Goodbye, Dora-Mittelbau. Goodbye, Savatzki Werke. Goodbye, Niemeier's shop and Nordhausen.

CHAPTER 10

Last Days of Captivity, Bergen-Belsen

Our evacuation train was moving, generally speaking, north. Its maneuvering resembled that of a boat sailing against the wind, going west then east sometimes and even south. Nevertheless, we inched up to the north. We crossed many towns and stopped at many railroad stations. I only remember a few of their names: Herzberg, Hildesheim, Haldensleben, Gardelegen, Salzwedel, Uelzen, and Soltau. It was truly amazing that this train kept moving. Germany was in agony from the almost incessant bombing. The roar of artillery fire was audible to the southwest. Decimated military detachments crossed the country in a disorganized manner. Thousands of refugees were at depots. Railroad tracks and telephone lines were interrupted. Yet fanatical SS officers forced their trains through just to fulfill their orders.

Apparently, using their own communication system, they traced a possible route to a town located further north and ordered the train operators to send the train that way. Sometimes, however, a railroad intersection ahead of our train was bombed and destroyed. So we backed up to the intersection behind us, and a new route was chosen. Other times, we had to wait until the tracks in front of us were repaired.

Several times, while stopped at a station, an air attack went overhead. This was no fun whatsoever. We the prisoners had to remain in our cars whereas the SS guards took shelter in land crevices surrounding the station. Throughout this journey, we were very careful to hide our food from the SS and other prisoners. With the help of our guardian angels, we were very frugal in consuming our bread. When everybody else ran out of their supply, we still had plenty. During the last day of our journey, it was a big problem, how to secure our bread from being grabbed by our hungry comrades. But then after long months of terror, we were fighting for survival. Humanitarian impulses by this time were extremely rare, reserved perhaps to only one: Father Maximilian Kolbe.

From Soltau, our train was sent south to another infamous concentration camp: Bergen-Belsen. Was it the original destination of our transport? I doubt it! Bergen-Belsen was overloaded with prisoners, living and dead. There was no room for even one more Häftling. This was obviously known to the SS authorities. The rumors circulated that the intention was to drown us in the sea near Lübeck. Now, since the continuation of our journey north was no more possible, they decided to dump us off in Bergen-Belsen. However, even access to this camp was blocked by piles of cadavers, and an epidemic of typhus or typhoid fever was raging inside. So even the SS did not want to be near it. Finally, they took us to the military barracks, which were close by. These barracks were part of an enormous facility consisting of maybe one hundred masonry buildings, intended to house soldiers participating in sharpshooting exercises. This smaller group of buildings was located on the eastern edge of a large square range approximately ten miles by ten miles. On the western edge was a much larger barracks facility called Fallinbostel.

They did not let our train enter the rail yard, which was inside the concentration camp. It stopped in a field very close to the military barracks. After jumping out of the cars, we did not have to walk very far. However, getting out of the cars without a platform was very difficult, especially for those hungry, weak, and exhausted by the terror of that four-day journey. Many hurt themselves in the process and remained lying on the ground, incapable of moving any further. Later, after those capable moved away, these victims were all shot dead by the SS, and the corpses hauled to the piles within camp Bergen-Belsen by local Häftlinge.

We were packed into several masonry buildings or blocks at a rate of two Häftlinge per bed. I was with Edek in a bed on the lowest level of three. Above us was my friend from Dora—Stan Lipinski—and his new buddy—Joe Chybinski; both were engineers and in terrible physical shape. I gave them the rest of my crumbled bread. They had traveled in another car of our train, so our meeting on this block was quite accidental. Stan, as I mentioned before, was arrested in Warsaw immediately after the uprising whereas Joe was captured in Grenoble, France, where he was studying electrical engineering. He spent about a year in a German concentration camp located in France then was brought to Dora. From this point, they became my best friends and remained so for many years to come.

The last eight days of our slavery were extremely boring and hungry. It was relatively easy for the SS command to maintain order in this provisory camp. Very few of us were able to move around the camp. We just lay in our beds and daydreamed that the Allies were close and would be here in a few hours or tomorrow. Of course, from time to time, the SS men ordered their beloved roll calls. It was more for our "entertainment" than for any practical purpose. They seldom counted us, which usually was the prime reason for the Appell. The bodies of dead prisoners were carried out of the block early in the morning, and by 8:00 a.m., a death Kommando from Bergen-Belsen arrived and collected them. Nobody counted these bodies either.

During this week, it was only about four or five times that we got something to eat—two times a piece of bread and two or three times Auschwitz-like soup. There was plenty of *ersatz* coffee, which I did not drink. It is truly amazing how little a human being needs to survive when not losing energy for some kind of activity.

Slowly the number of SS personnel was shrinking. By the end of the week, only about two dozen remained. Over a hundred had disappeared. Those who decided to stay were the least harmful of all of them. As a general rule, nobody saw them terrorizing the prisoners. We did not even know what their original duties in the camp were. The only brutes remaining in our camp were a few Blockältester and

Kapos. Those mostly were ordinary criminals brought to the concentration camp from prisons in Germany as well as from other countries occupied by Nazis. No matter what origin or nationality, 90 percent of them were outlaws.

Our impending liberation did not seem very exciting. In fact, there was a certain amount of apprehension about what the future would bring! However, considering it from the perspective of time, it was due. On April 15, 1945, around noon, we heard the crunch of tank tracks on the road behind our blocks. Those who could move ran to the windows or to the outside. Immediately electrifying news spread through the camp: "British tanks on the road!" Yes, they were there; they bypassed our camp, and they were gone! And there was quiet again—no action, no movement. Then at about 4:-00 p.m., two jeeps arrived and entered our barracks area. One carried heavily armed soldiers, and the other one a few officers. They circled the barracks then stopped in front of the building occupied by the SS troops. A white flag was projecting from one of the windows, and a few SS men came out with their hands up. But after the Englishmen said a few words, the Germans relaxed. They answered some questions, then the British officer issued an order that was accepted with an obedient yet happy shout: "*Jawohl, Herr Major!*"

Now the two jeeps proceeded through the entire barracks, announcing by the loudspeaker, "From now on, this camp is taken over by His Majesty's Army Division and Regiment [whose names or numbers I do not remember]. We will take care of you to the best of our abilities. However, we ask you to maintain order. In the next few days, a new administration will be set up, but for the time being, everything shall remain as is. Do not attempt to leave the camp. German guards will remain at their posts until tomorrow."

This was repeated time and again in English and in German, cooling our joy and enthusiasm. The jeeps drove away, and for the first night of our liberty, we remained hungry and still guarded by Germans.

If we were somewhat stronger, most likely, we would not have submitted to this rule. But we were so weak, so exhausted, that one could do anything to us without any resistance.

The next morning, British military kitchens arrived and proceeded to distribute soup. It was some kind of gruel, nothing substantial—disappointing again. They brought this soup to each of the blocks and made an effort that everybody got a share, even those who could not get out of their beds. It was very difficult to prevent smart guys from taking a second or third helping. When the commotion of soup distribution was over, we noticed that our barracks were surrounded by a tight cordon of soldiers clad in khaki-brown uniforms. As it became known, those were Hungarians, whose regiment was stationed in a distant section of this enormous facility.

Hungary was a lukewarm ally of Germany against the Soviet Union, but they refused to fight against the Western Allies. So the Germans kept them in semi-internment. The British found them useful in keeping concentration-camp prisoners inside the camp.

Our disappointment deepened! There was no liberty and no appreciable food, and our enemies still had the upper hand. The unrest and dissatisfaction were spreading. In particular, the Russians complained bitterly and loudly. In the afternoon, more British officers arrived. They finally disarmed the SS men and declared them to be the prisoners. All military insignia was stripped off their uniforms, belts taken away, and white armbands provided. They became known as the camp's housework Kommando. Then a temporary internal administration board was appointed. It consisted of representatives from various nationalities of just liberated prisoners. Those who spoke English were preferred. Before sunset, they brought in another light meal, which restored some energy to many of our fellows.

While still surrounded by the Hungarians, many of the inmates began to plunder within the barracks. They succeeded in breaking into a warehouse with military medical supplies. There they found a quantity of bottles with alcohol. Some contained good, drinkable grain alcohol (C_2H_5OH). Many other bottles, identical in size and shape, were methyl alcohol (CH_3OH), which is poison. They were marked as such with a skull and crossbones symbol and with the chemical formula as well. But many disregarded the warnings, and around fifty inmates died. Somebody brought a bottle to our room. We diluted it with water and drank a toast "to our liberty" from our tin cups. This stuff, fortunately, was not poisonous. Then during the night, a mob of radicals, burning with vengeance, lynched many former Kapos and Blockältester. The next morning, completely by accident, I wandered into the loft space where many of the hangings took place and saw a number of those mutilated bodies. What a horror! What a macabre! What merciless savagery!

Our former overlords, ex-SS men, now working hard, had to collect all these cadavers and bury them in more or less a decent manner somewhere outside the camp.

It now became evident that we had to organize ourselves in a hurry to establish some law and order within our demoralized and confused community. It was not a simple matter since animosities between the numerous nationalities started to wreak havoc. The British didn't want to and really couldn't mix into our internal problems.

Fortunately, various liaison officers started to show up and took care of their nationals. The Belgians, Dutch, and Norwegians had been removed in several trucks, escorted by their soldiers, on April 17. The next day, a much larger convoy took the French group. Then the Soviet mission arrived. They protested the Hungarian guards and demanded an immediate separation of their citizens from the other ex-prisoners. The British disagreed, wanting to leave it as it was. The arguments ended with a compromise. Soviet officers were permitted to issue passes to their subjects whom they considered trustworthy of nonviolent behavior outside of the camp. In no time, sizeable groups of Russians under the leadership of dedicated communists started to go out. They returned after several hours, loaded with all kind of goods—food in particular—robbed from the farmers in the neighborhood. Naturally, the other folks in the camp became unhappy and unruly. So the British agreed to segregate the Soviets from the rest, but now it became apparent that not all Soviet citizens were willing to move into their new section. Those reluctant were forced to move by their fellow citizens as well as by the Soviet mission officers and, ultimately, by the British MPs. The few who spoke Polish insisted that they were citizens of Poland and remained with the Poles. However, our future was still uncertain too. Fortunately, the Western Allies still recognized the Polish government in exile (residing in London) as legal representatives of all Poles. The liaison officers were actually delegates of that government. They did whatever they could to prevent forcible repatriation. And quick repatriation of everybody was very much on the Britons' mind. In fact, they hated the Poles for our overwhelming rejection of being sent to our fatherland, which was already in the grip of the Red Army, which was setting up a puppet regime composed entirely of communists.

Instead, our Polish delegates arranged to have all the remaining inmates (including the Russians) ultimately transferred to much better accommodations across the range in Fallinbostel.

From day to day, our food rations improved slightly. There was plenty of water for drinking and washing. Then the Red Cross arrived with civilian clothing. Finally, we got rid of those horrid striped uniforms. On April 22 or 23, the Hungarian guards disappeared. We were free. Free!

I joined a group of young men, and we wandered around the countryside for several hours mostly for the joy of our newfound freedom than for any practical purpose. Nevertheless, we brought back a small (about forty pounds) pig. It was roasted over the campfire. What a feast it was! I was not famished anymore! By now, our barracks housed almost exclusively citizens of prewar Poland. There remained, however, a few Byelorussians, Gypsies, Jews, and Ukrainians. Stan Lipinski and Joe Chybinski joined the camp's board of administration, and I was asked to serve in the camp police. We succeeded in organizing the life in our camp in an orderly manner. Then we were told that we would have to accommodate additional Polish people in our barracks. These Poles were mainly persons brought to Germany to work in factories and farms—so-called free laborers.

Among them was the young lady who became my wife, Leonarda Mierzwa. She succeeded in staying in her native Poland until the Soviet army approached. To avoid the "Red liberation," with the blessing of her mother, she escaped to the west, traveling with the German family for whom she worked as a nursemaid for their children. For me, her appearance was like the first rays of the rising sun, bringing light, warmth, and hope. Together, it was so much easier to leave behind all the past miseries and look to an unknown future... but a future of freedom.

Epilogue by Andrew Haszlakiewicz

Four weeks after first laying eyes on each other, my parents married. The date was May 25, 1945, when Zbyszek and Lonia embarked on an incredible life journey together, which lasted sixty-two years.

At the conclusion of WWII in Europe, the provisional German government established several programs for the restitution of displaced persons within their borders. One such program offered free higher education and housing for qualified individuals. My dad qualified, and by the time I arrived in September 1946, he was enrolled in the Braunschweig Polytechnic School.

By the time Zbyszek completed his degree in urban planning in the spring of 1951, the political and economic climate in Poland precluded his return home. Instead, the family of three immigrated to the USA and settled in Chicago, Illinois. Two years later, in 1953, my sister Basia was born.

Throughout his adult life, my dad worked hard. Initially, of course, the hardest was surviving the Nazi horrors. Then came the building of a family and a career, which had their own ups and downs. During the 1950s, he worked as a draftsman and went to night school to earn a degree in structural engineering. In the '60s, working for a large architectural company in Chicago, he advanced to become Chief Structural Engineer and the head of the department. During this time, the company sent him to Poland to oversee large building projects—primarily meat processing plants.

Before the decade finished, my parents were able to move to Wilmette, a highly desirable northern suburb of Chicago on the shores of Lake Michigan. Hard work had paid off! The '70s found my dad forming his own engineering company and completing more projects in Poland. Working within the Polish communist structure at that time was very hard. However, this was a challenge he enjoyed, and he took great pleasure in outwitting the communist bureaucracy to complete numerous projects.

Leonarda Mierzwa, known as Lonia, was born and raised in western Poland, on the opposite side of the country from my dad. Both families were well off with land, livestock, and large homes with nannies and servants. All of that vanished in the fall of 1939. My mom, by virtue of having learned German, spent most of the war years working for a German family as a nanny to their three children. At the war's end, she found herself in Fallingbostel, Germany, working as a youth counselor. There she met my dad.

My mom was the ballast and keel to the ship that was my dad. She encouraged and supported him every step of the way. For ten years in the '50s and '60s, she worked for Sears, Roebuck and Co. so they could afford to move to Wilmette in 1967. Once there, her health faltered, and she became a homemaker, helping with my children in the late '70s and early '80s.

In 1987, my dad reached sixty-five years of age and retired. He and my mom moved to Florida, where, for the next twenty-one years, they enjoyed the Sarasota sunshine with many friends and family. During those years, five grandchildren—my sister's two (Olivia and Eleanor) and three from my side (Eric, Caroline, and Julie)—would visit on holidays and school breaks.

During the entire time of his retirement, Zbyszek stayed active, playing tennis regularly and busy, consulting as a structural engineer on many projects. His last project went unfinished.

Pancreatic cancer took my mom on January 6, 2008. Eighteen months later, on June 30, 2009, lung cancer claimed my dad. It was a remarkable life for both of them.

Note

My dad wrote this book during the mid-'90s and self-published it in 1998. With all due respect for those who helped him, it was not edited very well. Although spelling errors were few, there were a number of syntax errors and awkward sentence structures and passages. I took the opportunity of the COVID-19 pandemic lockdown of 2020–21 to reedit his manuscript. The final polishing of the text was done by Page Publishing, for which I am most grateful.

This year marks the one-hundredth year of my father's birth—August 19, 1922. His legacy is being honored with this new edition of *Madness of the XX Century*.

Andrew G. Haszlakiewicz
Wilmette, Illinois, 2022

Glossary of Terms Used in Concentration Camps

Antreten. To rally
Appell. Roll Call
Arbeitsstatistik. Labor (employment) office
Außen Kommando. Detachment working outside camp
Badeanstalt. Bath facility
Block. Dormitory barracks
Blockältester. Prisoner in charge of one barracks
Bunker. Prison within a concentration camp
Entlausung. Getting rid of lice
Führer. Leader or commander
Gestapo. Geheime Staatspolizei; Secret State Police
Häftling(e). Prisoner (inmate), prisoners
Homosexual. Homosexual Pervert (Para, 175 German Penal Code)
Kommando. Work detachment or group
Kapo. Prisoner in charge of a work detachment
Lager. Camp
Lagerältester. Prisoner in charge of an entire camp
Lager Dolmetscher. Official camp interpreter
Lagerschutz. Camp security
Links um. Turn left
Mützen. Cap
Mützen ab. Caps off
Mütze auf. Caps on
Muselman(en). Rundown prisoner (walking skeleton)
Obersturmführer. SS officer rank: lieutenant
Raus. Get out

Rechts um. Turn right
Revier. Concentration camp hospital
Schreiber. Scribe, clerk
Scharführer. SS NCO rank: corporal
Stubendienst. Barracks or room serviceman
Sturmbannführer. SS officer rank: major
Töten Kommando. Death detachment
Transport. Transport
Untersturmführer. SS officer rank: second lieutenant
Vorarbeiter. Foreman, working group leader
Waescherei. Laundry
Zugang. Incoming transport of prisoners

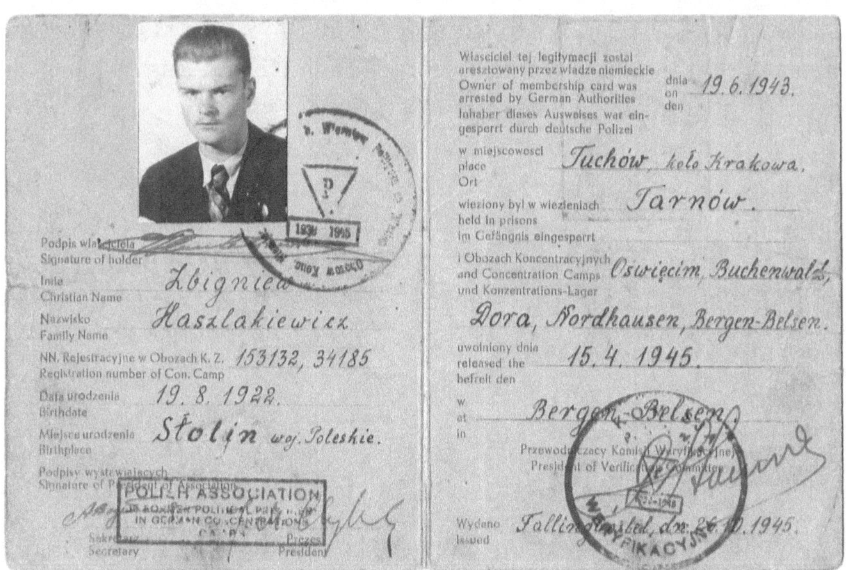

Photo I.D. issued 6 months after liberation.

ABOUT THE AUTHOR

Zbigniew Marian Haszlakiewicz was born into wealthy Polish nobility on August 19, 1922, in Stolin, Poland (now Belarus). His life of privilege began to unravel in 1930 when his father died and stopped altogether when his mother died in 1932. Orphaned at the age of ten, he was taken in by an uncle and his wife to a farm 100 miles south to what is now Ukraine. He had just begun his final year of secondary school in 1939 when World War II broke out. The family of three escaped the Soviet incursion by finding shelter in south-central Poland. It is there, in the spring of 1943, the author's two-year ordeal began with his capture by the Nazis Gestapo.

After being liberated by the British in 1945, Mr. Haszlakiewicz remained in Germany, married, started a family, and earned a degree in Urban Planning from the Braunschweig Polytechnic. In 1951, the family of three emigrated to the U.S. and settled in Chicago, IL, where he had a successful career as a structural engineer. After retiring to Florida in 1987, family and friends convinced him to write down what he experienced in the Nazis concentration camps. The original edition of "Madness of the XX Century" was self-published in 1998. Zbigniew Marian Haszlakiewicz died in 2009. He was 86 years old.